"A gap in therapy for ADHD has been beautifully addressed by this program for managing executive functioning deficits in the college student population. The authors, all experts in adult ADHD, have distilled their years of clinical research and expertise into a finely honed program for this college population desperately in need of assistance with the high executive functioning demands of today's college environment. This highly useful program will be a necessary resource for anyone working with this ADHD population."

Russell A. Barkley, Ph.D., *Clinical Neuropsychologist, Retired. Author,*
Taking Charge of ADHD *and* Taking Charge of Adult ADHD

"This program is such a great resource! It takes the foundational skills that have been validated in adults and in high school students and applies them to the unique needs of college students where there are many life-transition milestones. Modules including 'adulting', substance use, balancing independence with looping in parents, and setting the stage for next steps in the workplace make this set of skills unique and highly relevant. I would highly recommend this program to any clinician working with college students coping with a full-fledged diagnosis of ADHD or with related symptoms."

Steven A. Safren, Ph.D., *Professor of Psychology, University of Miami. Author,*
Mastering Your Adult ADHD: A Cognitive-Behavioral Treatment Program

"*Thriving in College with ADHD* is exactly what clinicians are looking for. This is the right program at the right time for the field. The Therapist Guide offers a modular structure grounded in rigorous science with flexibility to meet individual client needs. The accompanying Student Workbook for clients is inviting and user-friendly with accessible language and relatable examples. The package helps clinicians transform science into action. Exactly what university counseling centers need right now."

Julie S. Owens, Ph.D., *Professor of Psychology and Co-Director*
of the Center for Intervention Research in Schools, Ohio University

THRIVING IN COLLEGE WITH ADHD

Developed by four professors who also happen to be experts in attention-deficit/hyperactivity disorder (ADHD), this interactive and customizable workbook provides coaching to students with ADHD to make skills like managing time, motivating and organizing oneself, and "adulting" a workable part of everyday college life.

Other books for college students with ADHD only describe personal experiences or just give advice, but this workbook promotes learning through interactive exercises and behavioral practice. It will allow you to address issues most relevant to your needs at whatever pace feels right. Modules are designed to be engaging, digestible, and activity-oriented. With practice, you will come away with improved skills that will help you to succeed in college and to live your best life. This workbook can be used on its own; however, an accompanying *Thriving in College* guide for therapists uses an approach that mirrors what you will be learning and doing. If you have this workbook and are getting support from a therapist, encourage them to use the therapist guide along with you!

Parents can also benefit from information in this workbook, to help their college students along the way and to understand ADHD and how it impacts the college years.

Laura E. Knouse, Ph.D., is Professor of Psychology at the University of Richmond. She is an expert in CBT for adult ADHD and study skills for college students with ADHD.

Will Canu, Ph.D., is Professor of Psychology at Appalachian State University. His research focuses mainly on ADHD in adulthood, including adjustment, assessment, and interventions.

Kate Flory, Ph.D., is Professor of Psychology at the University of South Carolina. She studies social, emotional, health, academic, and other outcomes among children, adolescents, and young adults with ADHD.

Cynthia M. Hartung, Ph.D., is Professor of Psychology at the University of Wyoming. She studies the assessment and treatment of ADHD in adolescents and emerging adults and sex/gender differences in psychopathology.

Thriving in College with ADHD

A Cognitive-Behavioral Skills Workbook for Students

**Laura E. Knouse, Will Canu,
Kate Flory and Cynthia M. Hartung**

Routledge
Taylor & Francis Group

NEW YORK AND LONDON

Cover image: © Getty Images

First published 2024
by Routledge
605 Third Avenue, New York, NY 10158

and by Routledge
4 Park Square, Milton Park, Abingdon, Oxon, OX14 4RN

Routledge is an imprint of the Taylor & Francis Group, an informa business

Library of Congress Cataloging-in-Publication Data
A catalog record for this book has been requested

ISBN: 978-0-367-71167-2 (hbk)
ISBN: 978-0-367-71163-4 (pbk)
ISBN: 978-1-003-14962-0 (ebk)

DOI: 10.4324/9781003149620

Typeset in Baskerville
by Apex CoVantage, LLC

Contents

Acknowledgments

We express our sincere gratitude to the graduate students in our labs and on our practicum teams who helped to lead the therapy groups on which this approach is based. We also wish to thank our clients whose hard work and insights have informed this work and made it better. We also thank Alex Fossum for her assistance with graphic design and manuscript formatting.

—The Authors

Many thanks to my undergraduate research students who gave helpful feedback on my draft material during the completion of this work and to the University of Richmond for their support via a School of Arts and Sciences Faculty Summer Research Fellowship and a Faculty Fellowship from the Office of the Provost.

—LEK

Thank you to Rebekah for all of your support and encouragement, and thank you to Owen and Sophia for being my Sun and Moon. You inspire me, and I love you all more than words can say.

—WC

Special thanks to the University of South Carolina College of Arts and Sciences for their support via a Book Manuscript Finalization Award. All my love to my family, Neil, Carter, and Austin, who support me fully in everything that I do.

—KF

I am grateful to my graduate students, Christopher, Patrick, Anne, Judah, John, and Tamara, who contributed their ingenious ideas to this program over the years. Working with you all is the best part of my job. Love and thanks to Billie and Ben, who have both appreciated and tolerated my planning skills, especially during their school years when they allowed me to try out many of these techniques with them and gave me honest feedback.

—CMH

Introduction

Understanding ADHD and Workbook Overview

I Have ADHD: What Does That Mean?

Maybe you were diagnosed with attention-deficit/hyperactivity disorder (ADHD) as a child and all you were told by your parents was that taking medication would help you do better at school. Maybe you went to the doctor as a teenager and mentioned struggling with grades and focusing in class and your doctor wrote a prescription for Adderall or another medication.

Whether you know little about ADHD or feel like you are pretty well informed, it can be helpful and empowering to review what having ADHD means, *especially* for succeeding in college.

ADHD is a disorder with three core symptom areas: inattention, hyperactivity, and impulsivity. Hyperactivity and impulsivity are often grouped together in talking about ADHD symptoms. In addition, ADHD often involves difficulty with feeling and acting on strong emotions (which is known clinically as emotional dysregulation). It is important to note that not everyone with ADHD has symptoms from all of these areas. For example, some people only have symptoms of inattention, which in earlier decades was referred to as attention-deficit disorder or ADD. Others have symptoms from two or even all three categories (see Table 0.1 for examples).

As you probably already know, it is also important to understand that, in ADHD, the symptoms of inattention, hyperactivity-impulsivity, and emotional dysregulation are *chronic* (they are a pattern for you) and *impairing* (they cause problems for you). People with ADHD usually start experiencing these symptoms in early childhood, and they often cause problems across many areas, including (a) school, (b) work, (c) family, friend, and (later on) romantic relationships, (d) leisure and sports activities, (e) money management, and (f) risky behaviors, that later in life include unsafe driving, risky sexual behavior, and drug and alcohol use problems. One thing that may vary over time is the amount of difficulty that these symptoms cause for you. For example, some people might have done okay in elementary school but encountered more difficulty in middle school or high school. A delay in the appearance of difficulties might happen when, for example, a child has a teacher who is very in-tune with the child's strengths and weaknesses and provides some informal accommodations (like extra time for homework assignments).

One thing that we also know about ADHD is that having it *does not mean you cannot succeed in your life!* We personally know lots of people who have dealt with ADHD and gone on to complete college, graduate school, become leaders in their field, and so on, and there are tons of others who are in the public eye who have ADHD, too. Michael Phelps and Simone Biles,

DOI: 10.4324/9781003149620-1

Table 0.1 Core symptoms of ADHD.

Symptom Area	Definition	Example
Inattention	Often having difficulty following clearly delivered instructions, losing track of the topic in conversations, or being distracted by things in the environment that are not central to the task at hand.	You are trying to finish your homework for class tomorrow but can't stay focused. You are distracted by your phone, friends working nearby, and pretty much everything around you.
Hyperactivity-impulsivity	Problems like often blurting out responses before a question has been fully posed, making decisions without thinking about all the possible consequences, and feelings of restlessness that often result in fidgeting.	You have a lot of trouble sitting through a lecture or standing in line because you would rather be moving around. You often make quick decisions that you later regret. You interrupt others or blurt out answers in class more often than your classmates.
Emotional dysregulation	A tendency to react quickly and intensely to your emotions.	Your friend makes a comment that you find offensive. You become instantly upset, curse your friend, and storm off.

world-famous US gold-medal Olympians? Yep, they have ADHD. Dave Grohl, Foo Fighters front-man? Has ADHD. Emma Watson, amazing actor and Ivy-league graduate? You guessed it, she has ADHD, too. So does Ryan Gosling. Silicon Valley giant and billionaire Bill Gates, and IKEA founder Ingvar Kamprad have "gotten by" while having ADHD, as well. While these are clearly exceptional individuals, they prove a point: Just because you have ADHD does not mean you should sacrifice your dreams. And if those dreams involve finishing a college degree, well, we're here to help!

What Causes ADHD?

The root causes and underlying mechanisms of ADHD have been the subject of much research. Two factors have received the most support: (a) biological and genetic factors that are thought of as *causes* of ADHD, and (b) environmental factors that *exacerbate* (make worse) symptoms of ADHD. Table 0.2 highlights the causal and exacerbating factors for ADHD.

Who Has ADHD and Do They Grow Out of It?

One well-known truth about ADHD is that there is a gender difference in who is affected. Research has shown that boys are about two-to-three times more likely than girls to be diagnosed with ADHD. The difference is smaller in adults (three men for every two women). Girls and women with ADHD are more likely to experience inattention, while boys and men with ADHD often have more problems with hyperactivity and impulsivity. Unfortunately, this often leads to later identification of girls or women with ADHD, who are frequently the "daydreamers" in elementary school but don't disrupt the class or perform too poorly in academics. Boys with ADHD more commonly engage in impulsive behaviors (e.g., pushing another student down to reach for an eraser instead of finding another) or hyperactivity (e.g., wandering into the hallway during a

Table 0.2 Things that cause ADHD or make it worse.

Factors	Examples
Causes	
Genetics	The heritability of ADHD is quite strong, similar to some physical characteristics, like height. ADHD is linked to genes involving neurotransmitter regulation in the brain.
Other biological factors	Lead exposure, complications at birth (like oxygen deprivation), and brain injury have been shown to lead to ADHD symptoms.
Might make it worse	
Nutrition	Not eating breakfast has been linked to poor concentration in school for children. Limited intake of specific nutrients may be also be linked to sub-par brain functioning.
Sleep	Sleep loss is linked to impaired task completion, inattention, and emotional dysregulation.
Stressors	Child or spouse abuse in the home (or other major family-related disruption) is linked to impulsivity, inattention, and dysregulated emotions. Stress can reduce your capacity to concentrate.
Environment fit	Roles that require multitasking and independent work will increase ADHD impairment. Tasks that are frequently reinforcing, like video games, will be easier for people with ADHD.

lesson), and therefore tend to be noticed and then referred earlier to health professionals or school staff for intervention. Have you been diagnosed with ADHD? If so, do you know how old you were when you were first identified as having ADHD?

You may have wondered about whether ADHD occurs only in the United States. Studies have been conducted now on every continent in the world, and while these have shown some differences in how many children and adults have ADHD across countries, the take-home message is clear: ADHD is a real disorder that is seen worldwide and has been documented by doctors since the late 1700s.

Finally, while we used to think that ADHD only occurred in children and adolescents, it is now understood that ADHD often continues into adulthood. In fact, it is not very unusual for ADHD to be first diagnosed in college, because symptoms were either not disruptive or at least not problematic enough to warrant professional attention, earlier. It is important to note that *all* people with ADHD (or their parents or siblings or teachers) should, however, be able to recall *some* problems with inattention, hyperactivity-impulsivity, and/or emotional dysregulation in childhood.

The way ADHD looks for adults can differ across individuals. Some people with ADHD have many symptoms and meet diagnostic criteria in both childhood and adulthood. Others have fewer symptoms as adults than they did as kids, and therefore only partially meet the "official" diagnostic criteria. However, many like this *still* experience daily problems related to their remaining symptoms. Still others are negatively affected by ADHD as children but either learn to cope with their symptoms as adults or choose careers that do not require too much concentration, so they seem like they do not really have ADHD anymore. And some children with ADHD – probably mainly in mild cases – do somehow seem to "grow out of" their symptoms. Which one of these describes your experience with ADHD?

So, How Does ADHD Affect College Students Like Me?

In people of all ages, the symptoms of ADHD usually occur along with what is known as executive functioning (EF) problems. Let's talk about EF and its impact on functioning in college. EF involves several specific cognitive (thinking) abilities related to *self-regulation*. These abilities include set-shifting (the ability to purposefully shift your attention back and forth between tasks), working memory (taking in, using, and manipulating information in your mind), inhibition (the ability to delay a response), and maintaining sustained attention (like you need in many activities that aren't "fun"). These abilities are the building blocks for planning and goal setting, completion of complex tasks that require lots of effort, and successful social interactions. EF also helps us to regulate our thoughts, feelings, and behaviors, and to manage our time and energy. All of these abilities are critical to success in college. So, it should be clear how people with ADHD who have problems with EF often also have difficulty in college.

The greatest challenge that *all* college students face is the complicated task of mastering independent living in a setting that is intellectually and organizationally challenging. Gone are the highly structured days of high school with a class scheduled every period, where parents, teachers, and administrators helped to keep you on task and in the right location and often provided special in-class learning assistance or at-home help with organization. This transition also means you will let go of the help provided by your parents or other guardians. No one is there to make you start and focus on homework after class. No one is there to ensure that steps are taken early enough to complete long-term projects. No one is there to provide money on a need-to-have basis. For any college student, assuming all of the responsibility that such independence entails can be difficult, if not overwhelming. *However, for those affected by ADHD and EF problems, all of this is so much harder.*

Consider a college freshman named Drew who has ADHD and difficulties with EF. Drew is very smart but has problems with staying organized and planning ahead. In elementary, middle, and even high school, Drew's parents oversaw his daily home schedule, including time for homework. They helped him plan for big school projects and schedule adequate time for studying for tests. Drew's teachers also helped him and the other students stay organized by breaking up long-term projects into smaller parts with deadlines and giving outlines for in-class lectures. Drew had a curfew, and his parents had rules for completing his schoolwork before he could hang out with friends.

In college, although he is intellectually capable of doing the work, Drew is falling behind in all of his classes. He has missed the deadlines for multiple assignments and has not studied for exams in advance, resulting in poor grades. Drew is also having trouble keeping his dorm room clean and organized; he often cannot find his textbooks or other materials that he needs for class. He is also having trouble staying focused and taking notes in class when the professors give unstructured lectures, which they often do. Finally, feeling discouraged about his school performance, Drew is finding it harder and harder to motivate himself to attend classes and study when there are so many other fun social opportunities with friends.

Perhaps some aspects of Drew's experiences are similar to yours in college so far. Perhaps you are just hoping to avoid these sorts of problems. Either way, you have come to the right place!

How Will This Workbook Help Me?

We (the authors of this workbook) are all college professors who teach and mentor undergraduate students. We are also licensed clinical psychologists who specialize in research on and treatments for college students with ADHD. Collectively, we have over 60 years of experience working with students like you. In this workbook, we have put together a set of skills that address the biggest problems that college students with ADHD and EF difficulties face. The skills we present are straightforward, although it will likely take practice to get them to be a solid part of your routine. The skills are based on research evidence about what helps youth and adults with ADHD, and our own clinical experience providing treatments to college students with ADHD. We have seen many college students with ADHD master these skills and make big improvements in their academics, personal relationships, and other aspects of their lives. We are confident that these skills will help you too!

How Do I Use This Workbook?

This workbook is organized into six skillset sections, each addressing a topic that is often challenging for college students with ADHD and EF problems. These topics include:

- organization and time management skills
- professional learner skills (like taking quality lecture notes and finding your ideal study space)
- skills for thinking and acting differently
- skills for taking good care of yourself (like getting good sleep, exercising, and reducing substance use)
- skills for building strong relationships
- skills for effective "adulting" (which includes life skills such as taking care of your money and your living space).

Take a look at the table of contents. As you will see, each skillset contains multiple modules, each of which addresses a very specific skill within that section topic. We've designed this book so that you can use it flexibly. If you are using this workbook with a therapist, you will work with them to plan out which skills to work on and in what order. If you are using the workbook on your own, you can select the skillsets and modules that seem most helpful to you or that best address the main problems you're facing in coping with ADHD. Or you can start from the beginning, and go skill by skill, module by module. It's up to you!

Either way, **we strongly recommend that you begin with Skillset 1 on Organization and Time Management, because these skills serve as a foundation for everything that comes after**.

Throughout the workbook, you will find lots of examples, worksheets, and activities. There are also some questions at the beginning of each skillset that will guide you in choosing the modules in that section likely to be most helpful for you. In addition, we've added a few "road signs" throughout the book to help you easily identify particular kinds of information. You can use the key below to learn more.

 *Caution!*

This symbol indicates a place where we want to warn you about a common challenge or particularly sticky issue related to using the skills in this book. When you see a caution sign, be sure to review the information and consider whether it applies to your situation.

Focus on Your Goals

We use this symbol when we think it might be helpful to remind yourself *why* you're striving to use the skills in this book. When the going gets tough, it can be helpful to remind yourself what your goals are – whether it's getting good grades, working more efficiently so that you have time to do things other than studying, or working more effectively to keep your stress level low. Be sure to complete the following section on motivation (Introduction part 2) – you'll need it as you work through the skills in this book.

 Support System

We use this symbol when we think there might be a useful source of help outside of this book. We'll explain the type of help available and talk about how to go about getting it.

 Go Deeper

We use this symbol when we have additional sources of knowledge we'd like to recommend about a particular topic. If you're curious to learn more, you can find it here. When possible, we'll include a link to resources that can be accessed online.

I have more questions about ADHD, treatments, or accommodations.

That's great! One way to take ownership over your ADHD is to learn all you can about it and how it can be treated or accommodated at school or at work. Here are some links to resources from Children and Adults with Attention-Deficit/Hyperactivity Disorder (CHADD) the largest ADHD advocacy organization in the United States. ADHD experts review this information and make sure it's up to date and accurate.

 Do I really have ADHD? How do I know if it's the right diagnosis for me?

Assessment and Diagnosis of ADHD in Adults: https://chadd.org/for-adults/diagnosis-of-adhd-in-adults/

What about medication?

Medication Management of ADHD in Adults: https://chadd.org/for-adults/medication-management/

Should I get therapy for my ADHD?

Cognitive Behavioral Therapy for ADHD in Adults: https://chadd.org/for-adults/cognitive-behavioral-therapy/

Should I get accommodations for ADHD in college or at work?

Legal Rights and Accommodations in Higher Education and the Workplace: https://chadd.org/for-adults/legal-rights-in-higher-education-and-the-workplace/

Get Motivated

Learning new things can be hard, so in this short section we'll use some solid psychology strategies to help you get "In It to Win It", so to speak. Throughout this workbook, we'll be asking you to try out some new things that may honestly feel clunky at first. You don't need to be perfect, but you do need to be willing to try out the skills in your real life and make changes if things don't work out the first time. The key is to tweak each skill so that it fits into YOUR life, and that can take some practice.

But maybe you're thinking, "Okay, I've tried to use tricks to work on my ADHD before and it hasn't worked for me", or you're worried about whether you'll be able to follow through. You may not trust the You of the Future to get it done.

There is some truth to the idea that ADHD itself can make follow-through more of a struggle. You didn't ask to have ADHD! But we also know from our experience working with college students like you *and* from scientific research that students like you **can** and **do** learn to use skills that help them thrive with their ADHD. These strategies aren't something you're born with; they're new habits that you can learn with practice. Our behaviors and even our brains can grow and change. Remember, like any new skill:

You Can Improve Your Ability to Manage ADHD

Since you've made it this far in your education, you've actually probably learned hundreds of new skills across your lifetime. Let's do a quick thinking and writing exercise about this. First, think of a skill that you've learned in your life as a result of practice. This could be an academic skill (reading, writing, or math) or one related to a sport, artistic, or musical pursuit.

A skill I've learned through practice is:

_____

How difficult was this skill to learn? Did you experience any setbacks? If so, describe them:

_____

_____

_____

How did you respond when you experienced these setbacks? What kinds of strategies or help did you use to move forward:

_____

_____

_____

Great! That's good evidence that you can do hard things. :)

Take Your Motivation Temperature

It's impossible to be equally motivated to do all the things all the time, so it can be helpful to reflect on your current motivation level before we get started. We're going to use a quick thinking exercise developed by psychologists who study what motivates people (Case Western Reserve University, 2010). Answer the following questions to uncover your sources of motivation.

How **important** is it to learn skills to better manage ADHD right now (Figure 0.1)? Choose a number:

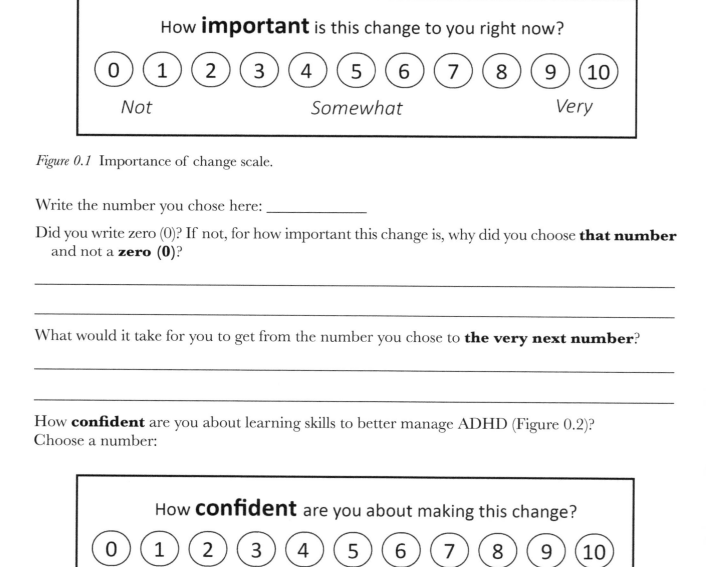

Figure 0.1 Importance of change scale.

Write the number you chose here: _____

Did you write zero (0)? If not, for how important this change is, why did you choose **that number** and not a **zero (0)**?

_____

_____

What would it take for you to get from the number you chose to **the very next number**?

_____

_____

How **confident** are you about learning skills to better manage ADHD (Figure 0.2)? Choose a number:

Figure 0.2 Confidence in change scale.

Write the number you chose here: _____

Did you write zero (0)? If not, for your confidence in making this change, why did you choose **that number** and not a **zero (0)**?

_____

_____

What would it take for you to get from the number you chose to **the very next number**?

_____

_____

Notice anything interesting about what came up in your responses? It's important to recognize that there's no "correct" level of motivation and that motivation is naturally going to go up and down over time – you've got a lot on your plate! But, if you feel your motivation waning, you can always come back to this exercise to tap into the reasons that making this change was – and might still be – important to you. And, you should also remind yourself of something we call:

Your Big Why

A Big Why is a "big picture", meaningful and personal reason why you want to make a change in your life. A Big Why isn't about simply getting papers turned in on time or getting good grades (although those things are nice!), it's about how you want to be in the world with respect to areas you value.

For example, think for a moment, in each of these areas, could your life be different if you were able to better manage ADHD? If so, how?

- Family Relationships
- Friendships
- Intimate Relationships
- Life-Long Learning
- Life's Work
- Recreation
- Health and Well-Being
- Spirituality
- Community

We know this might seem like heavy stuff when all you're trying to do is make it through the day in college, but we firmly believe that learning the skills in this book can actually **help you live a more vital, meaningful life** – to actually thrive *with* your ADHD. And, when the going gets tough, it's these meaningful Big Whys that can really keep you trying again.

So, for you, right now, which area of life we just listed is most meaningful to you? Which area could grow the most if you were able to better manage ADHD? Write it here:

_____

Now, write down three ways that this area would "look different" if you could better manage ADHD:

1. _____

2. _____

3. _____

Congratulations! You've identified your first Big Why. We recommend that you flip back to this page anytime you need to remind yourself why you're on this journey to begin with. And, you can always repeat this exercise to identify new Whys as they emerge. Finally, throughout the workbook, we'll also remind **you** to remind **yourself** of your Big Whys using this symbol:

 Congratulations! Let's Get Started!

Reference

Case Western Reserve University. (2010). *Readiness Ruler.* Center for Evidence-Based Practices. https://case.edu/socialwork/centerforebp/resources/readiness-ruler

1 Organization, Time Management, and Planning

Module 1.0 Why It Matters and Roadmap

Organizational skills are about figuring out what you need to do when and then actually doing it. Strategies for organization and time management include effective use of personal planners, task lists, and prioritization techniques. With everything going on in college, these skills will be vital to your success as a student. But . . . it's rare that anyone actually *teaches* students how to do these things. People usually figure things out pretty haphazardly through trial-and-error. Organization and time management are hard for most college students. Unfortunately, for students with attention-deficit/hyperactivity disorder (ADHD) and executive functioning (EF) problems, these skills can be especially hard to learn and maintain. You have to balance new responsibilities, more independence, and probably lots of social opportunities. This means you have a lot that can distract you from developing better organizational habits.

The sooner you learn these skills and learn how to use them consistently, the greater the benefit. Some research has suggested that, with the right instruction and support, even middle schoolers can effectively implement organizational skills. And now with the help of this workbook and your willingness to try out some new strategies, so can you! But don't worry – learning some new skills won't take away all your spontaneity and spunk. Instead, being more organized and planful in your life will help you be less stressed with the demanding work in college and you can carry those helpful habits with you after graduation and into "The Real World".

Organizational skills help reduce unpleasant surprises. They provide a structure for you to keep track of when assignments are due and when exams will be happening so you can choose how to best use your time and energy. Organization can also help you to get past low motivation that you might experience to work on more complex assignments, like papers that require a lot of thought, research, and writing. This can be accomplished by breaking all the tasks and subtasks that are necessary for completion of such an assignment into manageable chunks. Students often find this a much easier path to completion because it provides a steady stream of accomplishment that is motivating and a to-do-next list that is not overwhelming.

While there's a seemingly endless list of organizational strategies that might be helpful, we've found that these key skills provide the most benefit:

- Adopt and consistently use a *calendar and task or to-do list system*
- Systematically *prioritize tasks* based on urgency and importance
- *Break tasks into smaller steps* to prevent procrastination and increase satisfaction
- *Reward yourself* for completing tasks using a "when-then" rule

DOI: 10.4324/9781003149620-2

How Good Am I at Organization Now?

ADHD impacts different people in different ways. For example, you might be great at using a planner to keep track of upcoming commitments, appointments, and tasks, but be really challenged in prioritizing work on important, long-term projects. So, step one for you is to do some self-assessment to identify where you actually *have* room to grow in terms of organizational skills before you proceed with the modules in this section.

Self-Assessment of Organizational Skills. Complete the following worksheet, based on how these apply to you on a day-to-day basis in recent memory (about the last six months). Circle one response per item, using this scale: **0 = Never, 1 = Sometimes, 2 = Often, 3 = Very Often**.

1.	I have difficulty with attendance or being late at school or work	0 1 2 3
2.	I have difficulty keeping appointments (doctor, professor, etc.)	0 1 2 3
3.	I have trouble keeping track of when tests are scheduled or when assignments are due	0 1 2 3
4.	I have difficulty getting to bed at a reasonable time.	0 1 2 3
5.	I have problems getting ready to leave for the day.	0 1 2 3
6.	Others do important things for me (parents, friends, roommates, etc.)	0 1 2 3
7.	I have problems getting work done efficiently (completing assignments, etc.).	0 1 2 3
8.	I have problems getting started on tasks at school and/or work	0 1 2 3
9.	I have problems working to my potential (assignments are rushed or missing, etc.).	0 1 2 3
10.	I use the internet, social media, video games, or TV excessively or inappropriately.*	0 1 2 3
11.	I have problems keeping up with chores (laundry, dishes, shopping, etc.).*	0 1 2 3
12.	I have problems managing money (paying bills on time, sticking to my budget, etc.).*	0 1 2 3

Note: This workbook contains additional skills for these areas; however, we strongly recommend you complete Skillset 1 first because it builds a crucial foundation.

Alright, now that you have completed that inventory, there are a few different ways to look at the results. Each will give you different information about how your organizational skills work for you now.

First: Have you answered **more than two of the questions with a "2" or a "3"** (i.e., Often or Very Often – the grayed out numbers)? If so, this is a broad indicator that organization is something that you can improve, and that doing so may make a difference in your life. So, this Skillset is the right place for you. If you are reading this, the chances are that you have circled several answers in this range, but if not then you may want to consider focusing on other Skillsets in the book in order to maximize your immediate benefits.

Second: Consider your responses on items 1–3 (top section) and 4–12 (bottom section). Broadly, items in the top section correspond roughly to **keeping and effectively using a calendar** and items in the bottom section correspond to **prioritization, organization, and completion of tasks**. Look at the number of "2" or "3" responses you have in these areas. Having **one or more 2's or 3's in the top section**, means you may urgently need to focus on selecting and implementing a calendar and basic task list system (**Modules 1.1 and 1.2**). **Two or more 2's or 3's in the bottoms section** indicates you should learn skills to prioritize tasks and motivate yourself to complete them (**Modules 1.3, 1.4, and 1.5**).

Make Your Plan

Given what you have learned about (a) what organizational skills are and (b) how well you may "do organization" already, think about the following list of organizational modules, and check the ones you need to complete in the "In my plan?" column.

 In our experience, nearly ALL students could improve on their calendar and task list system, so we strongly recommend starting there.

Remember, you do not have to tackle these all at once! Take the modules one step at a time, because these skills really build on each other.

Organization and Time Management Skills Plan

In my plan?	Done	Module	Pages
		Module 1.1: Choose Your Calendar and Task List	**13–18**
		Module 1.2: Use Your Calendar and Task List Effectively	**18–25**
		Module 1.3: Set Your Priorities	**25–27**
		Module 1.4: Make Yourself Do Things	**27–32**
		Module 1.5: Get Unstuck From Procrastination	**32–38**

Module 1.1   Choose Your Calendar and Task List

The first and one of the most important steps to getting organized is to choose and begin using a calendar and task list system. Your calendar will help you keep track of your daily schedule and activities and manage your time, while your task list will be where you keep track of things you need to do, like assignments for school.

Most college students are really busy with classes, social events, clubs and organizations, internships, jobs, and other activities. You also have to fit in studying for exams, completing projects, doing errands and chores, exercising, seeing your family and friends, eating meals, and sleeping. You get the point! Many of these activities require multiple steps over an extended period of time and some require special materials.

Using a calendar and task list system is the key to getting organized and getting things done in all of these areas. It is very difficult to effectively organize, manage one's time, or plan for the future without a written (or electronic) record to work from. This is true for individuals without ADHD and EF problems, and especially true for those with these difficulties. Also, imagine how much "brain space" is used up by holding all these activities and tasks in your mind. Essentially, a calendar and task list can be thought of as a necessary lifeline when it comes to organization and time management. And, these tools can "free up brain space" so that you can be more efficient and effective in actually completing your activities and assignments.

You and Calendars

Do you currently use a <u>calendar system</u> to keep track of appointments, events, and due dates? If so, what kind of system do you use (e.g., paper planner, electronic calendar app) and how well is it working? If you don't currently use a calendar, have you ever used one? What was that like?

_____

_____

_____

Check Which of the Following Best Applies to You

☐ **My calendar system works SO WELL! I don't need to do anything differently**.

☐ **My calendar system works pretty well but I think I could make some improvements**.

☐ **I use a calendar system . . . sometimes. I definitely need to find a way to use it more consistently**.

☐ **I don't currently use a calendar system at all, but I'm willing to give it a try!**

Great! If your current system works SUPER WELL, then keep doing what you're doing! Otherwise, read on for tips on finding a good calendar system to try or re-committing to what you currently use.

You and Task Lists

Do you currently use a <u>task list</u> system to keep track of what things you need to remember to do? If so, what kind of system do you use (e.g., paper and pencil,

sticky notes, task list app) and how well is it working? If you don't currently use a task list, have you ever used one? What was that like?

_____

_____

_____

Check Which of the Following Best Applies to You

☐ **My task list system works SO WELL! I don't need to do anything differently.**
☐ **My task list works pretty well but I think I could make some improvements.**
☐ **I use a task list . . . sometimes. I definitely need to find a way to use it more consistently.**
☐ **I don't currently use a task list at all, but I'm willing to give it a try!**

If your current system works SUPER WELL, then keep up the good work! Otherwise, read on for tips on finding a good task list system to try or re-committing to what you currently use.

You may have tried using a calendar and task list in the past, but found they were not helpful. Often, we have discovered that when a calendar or task list system is not helpful for a student, it is because the student was not using it daily or for a long enough period of time for it to be helpful. Or, maybe the student was not including all of their important activities and assignments on the calendar and task list. In this chapter, we will guide you through selecting a calendar and task list system. In the next chapter, we will cover how to use your calendar and task list system effectively to get and stay organized.

If you have not had a good experience with using a calendar system in the past, you may have some concerns about life being "too scheduled" if you begin using a calendar. One thing we often tell our students who have this concern is that it is possible to both stick to a calendar and task list system and be spontaneous. For example, perhaps you will carefully schedule most hours of your weekdays in order to fit in classes, club activities, and your job. But, on the weekends, you will leave large blocks of time open for relaxation or "to-be-decided" activities, and in these times, you can be spontaneous. Or perhaps, on weekends, instead of scheduling all your tasks on your calendar, you create a to-do list of tasks that need to be completed before the weekend is over. Then, you fit these tasks around other activities that you spontaneously do. Even if you are skeptical of being "too scheduled", we urge you to give a calendar and task list system a fair try by working through this chapter and the next one. We bet you will find these tools to be as useful as we do!

Select Your Calendar System

Your calendar can be paper or electronic. Calendar systems commonly used by our students include paper-and-pencil planners, *Google Calendar, Outlook,* and *Apple Calendar.* Here (Figure 1.1) is an example of a college student's *Google Calendar. Outlook* and *Apple Calendar* look very similar.

One size does not fit all, so you should choose the best calendar system for you. However, one very important factor in choosing your system is that **it needs to be available to you at all times.** This is because updating and checking your calendar frequently is the best way to use it effectively.

Most college students have already developed the habit of having their phone with them at all times, and because of this we often encourage our students to pick a smartphone-based calendar app. Other benefits of this choice include the possibility of online or computer-based back-up for such calendars, most smartphone calendar apps are free, and also there's a lower likelihood of losing the calendar since you may be in the habit of keeping your phone with you already.

However, some students do not have smartphones or may simply prefer a paper-and-pencil calendar, and this is usually fine, as long as it is a size and format that will allow you to have it with you at all times in a pocket, a backpack, or a purse.

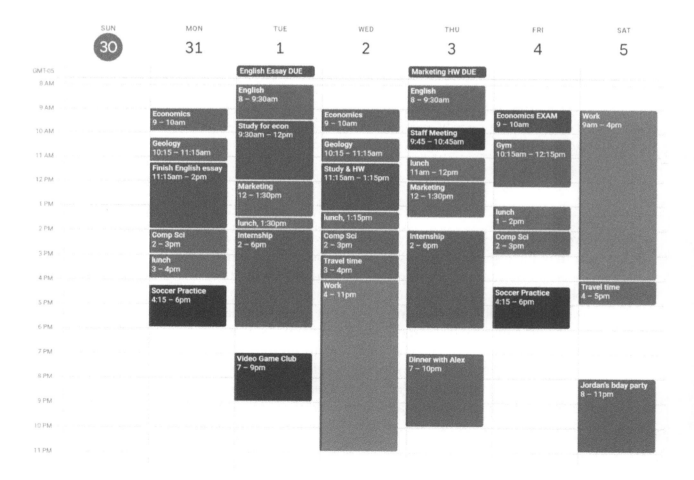

Figure 1.1 Example Google Calendar. Google and the Google logo are trademarks of Google LLC.

I'll Use A/An

☐ App-based calendar, specifically: _____

   ☐ Check here when you've downloaded the app and figured out how to pull it up on your computer, too

☐ Paper calendar

   ☐ Check here when you've purchased the calendar or ordered it online

Select Your Task List System

Your task list may be integrated with your calendar system (e.g., a list within *Outlook* or *Google Calendar*) or separate from it (e.g., a pad of paper or *Trello*). Task list systems commonly used by our students and colleagues include paper-and-pencil lists, dry-erase boards, *Trello, Google Keep, Google Calendar* list, *Apple Notes,* and *Apple Reminders.* See Figure 1.2 for an example of a college student's task list using *Trello.*

Again, the advantage of electronic lists is that they can be readily accessed. Applications like *Trello* are internet-based and can be accessed from any computer or smartphone. In addition, electronic calendar applications can double as a task list by entering tasks to be completed on the current day or later, depending on the urgency. For instance, one student noted that he schedules tasks as "all day" events in his electronic daily calendar, which tend to be highlighted and easy to see in the schedule and yet do not interfere with hour-to-hour appointments or activity listings. Such "events" (or, in this case, tasks) can also be set to repeat such that they appear every day until completed, when the student can delete future occurrences of the task.

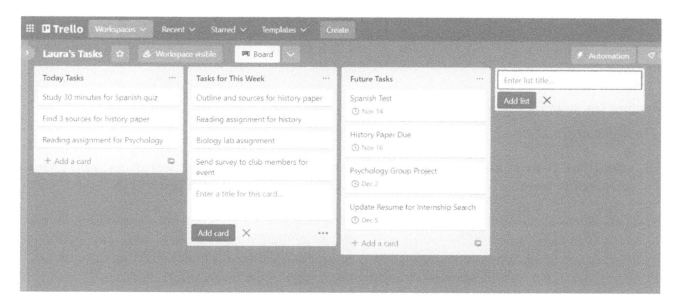

Figure 1.2 Example task list created with Trello. The authors are not affiliated with Trello and Trello does not endorse the contents of this workbook.

I'll Use A/An

☐ App-based task list, specifically: _____

    ☐ Check here when you've downloaded the app and figured out how to pull it up on your computer, too

☐ Paper task list

    ☐ Check here when you've gotten your paper list or ordered one online

Go for It!

In the next module, we will cover how to use your calendar and task list systems effectively to get and stay organized. In preparation, if you selected an electronic calendar and task list, download the applications onto your smartphone and computer and familiarize yourself with their formats before you begin the next module. If you selected a paper-and-pencil calendar or task list, purchase these items before you move ahead.

Regardless of which system you selected, in preparation for the tasks in the next module, begin collecting your class syllabi, club and activity schedules, work or internship schedules, and other listings of your required assignments, activities, and tasks. In the next chapter, we will review how to enter these items on your calendar and task list and how to use these new systems effectively.

Your Task List

☐ **Check here when you've got your calendar app or planner**
☐ **Check here when you've got your task list app or paper list**
☐ **Check here when you've gathered your class syllabi and other schedules into one place (paper folder or electronic folder)**

Module 1.2   Use Your Calendar and Task List Effectively

Welcome back! Now that you have chosen and gotten your hands on your calendar and task list systems, we're going to talk about how best to use them.

Setting Up Your Calendar and Task List

The **first step** is to:

☐ **add all of your regularly scheduled classes, appointments, meetings, and extra-curricular events (e.g., club meetings) to your calendar (Figure 1.3)**.

You can use your class syllabi and other materials you gathered after the last chapter to help with this task. You may believe that you do not need to include your *recurring* classes, appointments, meetings, and the like on your calendar since you might have your schedule for those memorized. However, there are two big benefits to adding these regular events to your schedule.

First, entering all classes, work or internship times, and regular appointments or meetings into the calendar is helpful for **making sure that you do not forget to go to these things!** Because ADHD and EF problems can make it hard to remember things and plan ahead, many students with ADHD forget to attend these regularly scheduled events even if they generally have their schedule memorized. Having these on your calendar serves as a reminder to attend, and also, for electronic calendar systems, you can set an alarm to remind you of an event that is coming up, say in 15 minutes. Do you sometimes lose track of time and forget to attend class or a meeting?

Second and maybe more importantly, entering these events on your calendar is critical for **being able to see how much time you have available to complete other things** on your task list before, after, or in-between classes or regularly scheduled appointments/meetings and, thus, learn to manage your time. For example, if you have a block of time open between classes, you might add to your schedule to study in the library for an upcoming test during that time.

Many students find it helpful to color-code events on their calendars by using a different color for each type of event. For example:

classes=blue
work=yellow
internship=red
extracurricular meetings=green

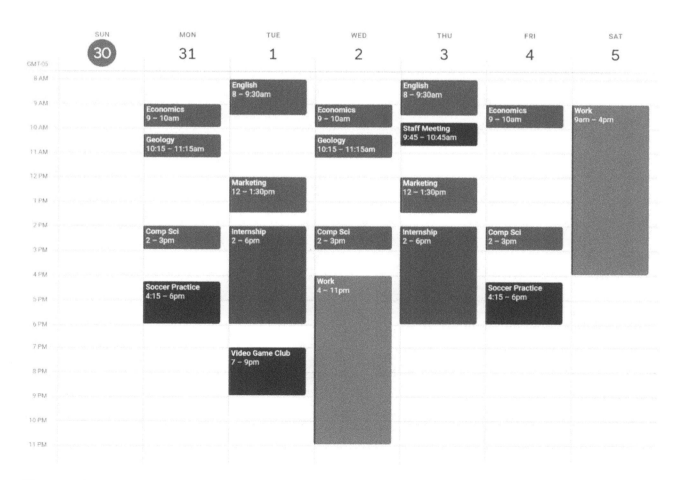

Figure 1.3 Calendar with recurring weekly events. Google and the Google logo are trademarks of Google LLC.

If you're using an electronic calendar, you don't need to enter repeated events individually. You can set the *recurrence* of these events – for example, adding your Chem 101 class at 10:30 every Tuesday and Thursday. Do a search for "how to set recurrence" for whatever calendar app you're using. Additional tip: You can also set the location of events or add a Zoom link right on the event so you'll have it when you need it!

Once you have entered all of your class meeting times and regularly scheduled commitments into your calendar, the **second step** is to:

☐ **transfer all exam dates and assignment due dates from your course syllabi to your calendar and also add them to your task list (Figure 1.4).**

If you are using an electronic calendar system, it works well to add these due dates as an "all day event" at the top of a day's calendar. Be sure to add a reminder notification or email! You should also add these items to your task list with due dates, starting with the ones that are coming up the soonest.

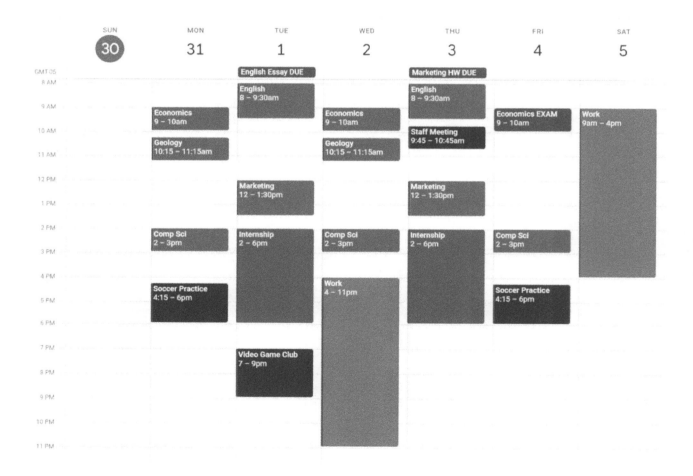

Figure 1.4 Calendar with assignment due dates at the top. Google and the Google logo are trademarks of Google LLC.

Once you have entered due dates for items required for your classes into the calendar, the **third step** is to:

☐ **schedule in regular study times and times to work on class assignments**.

For example, if you have weekly Spanish quizzes on Friday, you might schedule in blocks of time earlier that week for studying. Likewise, if you typically have papers due on Tuesdays, you might schedule writing time blocks several days prior. Right now, you might not have a very good sense of how much time you need to schedule to complete each project or study for an exam, but make your best guess and you can determine later if it was enough, too little, or too much time, and adjust your schedule moving forward.

For the <u>fourth step</u>, you should:

☐ **enter meal times, travel times, and times for exercise on your calendar as well as any non-recurring special events**.

This includes school breaks and social events with friends. Here is an example of what your final calendar for a given week might look like (Figure 1.5):

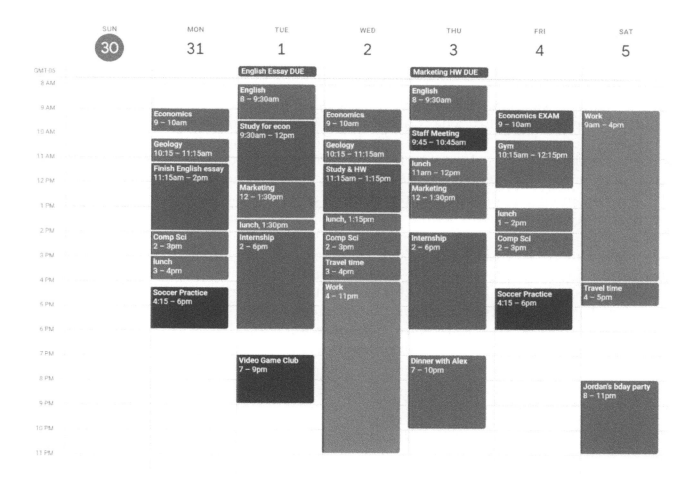

Figure 1.5 Example of final weekly calendar. Google and the Google logo are trademarks of Google LLC.

If you have not previously used a calendar and task list system, it may feel very overwhelming to begin entering information into these tools. This can be a process that takes some time, so we urge you to set aside a couple of hours to complete the task of setting up your calendar and task list systems. (Try to make it fun! Maybe you need a Scheduling playlist.) That way, you will not feel rushed or frustrated with how long it is taking. We have found that once students have gone through this process for one or two semesters, they are usually less overwhelmed with the task. And, the big payoffs are less stress, better readiness for tests and other assignments, and fewer missed opportunities.

Check Your Calendar and Task List Regularly

Now that you have created your calendar and task list systems, the **final step** is **checking and updating your calendar and task list regularly**. We typically suggest that you check and update these tools **at least three times per day**. To develop a habit of doing this, it is helpful to connect or "yoke" this to a daily activity (e.g., while drinking coffee in the morning, while brushing teeth at night). For example, a student might check their calendar and task list at night before going to bed to get an overview of what the next day will look like, again in the morning before leaving the house, and mid-day right after lunch. It does not matter exactly when you check your calendar and task list, as long as you get in the habit of referencing it several times a day.

Some students have found it difficult to remember to check their calendar and task list regularly despite yoking this to daily activities. In these situations, students have used other methods to remember to check their calendar and task list, including setting an alarm on their phone, keeping the calendar or task list open on their computer screen, or putting a sticky note on their refrigerator handle (to remind them to check before having breakfast in the morning and before dinner). No matter which strategies you use to regularly check your calendar and task list, we are certain that you will find these tools to be most useful when you do.

In addition to checking your calendar and task list regularly, **you should update your calendar immediately** when you schedule a new appointment, receive a new assignment, or think of something that needs to be completed. This is the best way to keep track of your schedule and be certain that you will not forget to attend an appointment.

I'll plan to check and update my calendar and task list daily at the following times (times of day OR while doing something you regularly do daily):

_____

_____

_____

☐ **Check here when you've set up reminders for these, if appropriate**.

Optimize Use of Your Calendar and Task List

In addition to checking and updating your calendar and task list system regularly, there are some ways to optimize your use of these tools:

1. Use Your Calendar to Keep Track of How Much Time Is Spent on Tasks

Many people have had the experience of tasks taking longer than planned. In addition, most of us have thought that there are not enough hours in the day to complete all of the things that we need to do. Individuals with ADHD and EF problems actually have more difficulty than others in estimating how much time has passed or how long it will take to finish something. Because unrealistic task-time estimates can sabotage students' effort to improve organizational skills and related academic performance (e.g., your motivation might decrease after repeated late- or all-nighters to finish tasks where the amount of time and effort needed were poorly judged), it may be most helpful to incorporate a time-tracking exercise early in your use of a calendar in order to inform your planning and time management.

Try keeping a log of how your time is spent over the course of a few days. For example, if you learn that making dinner, eating dinner, and doing the dishes consistently takes 45 minutes, then you will know how much time to allocate for that activity in the future. Likewise, if you learn that it takes approximately 4 hours to study for an exam to earn your desired grade, you will know to plan that much study time into your schedule for upcoming exams. You can actually use your calendar to log or track the time needed for a given task by adding these tasks to your calendar and then making notes about how long they actually took after the task is complete.

2. Reschedule Unfinished Tasks for Tomorrow

If you allocated two hours today to finish an English paper, but you were not able to complete it (either because the time was too short or for other reasons), you should schedule additional time in the next day or two to finish the paper. The rescheduling of unfinished tasks is a good activity to do when you look at your calendar at the end of each day and look ahead to the next day or two. This process of evaluating whether a task was completed, and if not, rescheduling it for tomorrow, will also help you to gain a better sense of how long it will take to complete similar tasks and assignments in the future.

3. Make Better Use of "Time Cracks" in Your Day

The term "time cracks", coined by psychologist Mary Solanto (2011), is used to describe relatively short periods of time (e.g., 10–30 minutes between classes or meetings) that can easily get spent on less meaningful activities (e.g., surfing the internet, checking social media, playing a mobile game). Use your calendar to notice when these time cracks occur and search your task list for items that will fit in the cracks and can be quickly completed. For instance, 20 minutes between classes could be used to schedule a dentist appointment, respond to an important email, review your budget, grab some lunch, or proofread an essay.

Some students schedule tasks on their calendar for their time cracks, or keep a separate "menu" of tasks that can be completed quickly during a time crack. Using time cracks wisely can help you to maintain a sense of accomplishment throughout the day and help you stay oriented to completing the tasks on your list.

Options for Filling Your Time Cracks

Check off any time crack fillers that seem useful to you and add your own. Be sure to copy these into a section of your calendar or task list.

☐ Review and rearrange the priorities on your task list
☐ Review your calendar for upcoming appointments
☐ Make a phone call (e.g., to schedule an appointment)
☐ Complete a "C" task from your list (see Module 1.3!)
☐ Study for an upcoming quiz
☐ Review the instructions for an upcoming assignment
☐ Write and email or text of gratitude to someone
☐ Make a grocery list or meal plan
☐ Organize your backpack or purse
☐ Unsubscribe from "junk" emails
☐ _____
☐ _____
☐ _____

Go for It!

Complete your calendar and task list according to the steps described in this module, and begin checking and updating them at least twice a day (three times is recommended). It is also encouraged that you try some of the additional strategies to optimize use of your calendar and task list that were introduced in this module.

☐ **Calendar and Task List Set-Up**

    ☐ **add <u>all</u> of your regularly scheduled classes, appointments, meetings, and extracurricular events (e.g., club meetings) to your calendar**

    ☐ **transfer all assignments, exam dates, and due dates from your course syllabi to your calendar and use these to set up your task list**

    ☐ **schedule in regular study times and times to work on class assignments**

    ☐ **enter meal times, travel times, and times for exercise on your calendar as well as any non-recurring special events**

☐ **Plan for Checking and Updating**

    ☐ **Check-in Times:**

        _____

        _____

        _____

    ☐ **Check here when you've set reminders for these times (if appropriate)**

☐ **Optimize Your Systems – Check Off the Strategies You Plan to Try**

    ☐ **Use your calendar to track how much time tasks take**

☐ **Reschedule unfinished tasks for the next day**
☐ **Make note of "time cracks" in your schedule and make a "menu" of possible time crack activities. Then do them!**

Module 1.3   Set Your Priorities

Looking at a full task list, it can be difficult to decide what to do first or when to start a task in order to complete it by the due date. To help out, you can **assign priority ratings** to the items in your task list and then tackle them in priority order. Task priority is usually determined by a combination of the **urgency** of the task (how soon must it be completed?) and the task's **importance** (how big of a deal is this task in terms of your overall life goals?).

The grid here shows how urgency and importance of a task can be considered together to determine your priorities (Figure 1.6).

Based on this grid, it is easy to realize that the tasks that are **urgent and important** (e.g., tests or academic assignments with deadlines in the next few days) should probably be completed first.

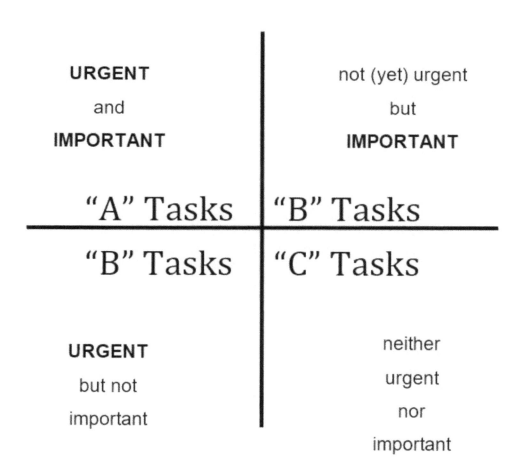

Figure 1.6 A model for task priorities.

So, like psychologist Steven Safren (Safren et al. 2017), we designate these as **"A" Tasks** in our priority system.

Tasks that are **important but not (yet) urgent** are ones that could wait a few days – for example, working on a big paper due in two weeks. However, these might also be good tasks to set aside some time in the next few days to get started on, even though they're not *yet* especially urgent. On the other hand, the tasks that are **urgent but not important** have an impending deadline, but they're not as important as "A" tasks. Taken together, we designate these middle-of-the road priority tasks as **"B" Tasks**.

Finally, we have our not-urgent-not-really-important **"C" Tasks**. Ahh . . . those "C" tasks. They're the ones that can sometimes suck up lots of time even though they're not going to move you toward your important goal. These tasks can make you *feel* like you're accomplishing something, especially when you might be avoiding getting started on a big, scary "A" Task or a daunting "B" Task. Examples of "C" Tasks might include tidying your room when you should be studying for finals, checking your email ONE MORE TIME, or "researching" something interesting on the internet.

It's time to practice setting priorities. **Take out the fresh, new task list you've set up and sort the items onto the grid in Figure 1.7**.

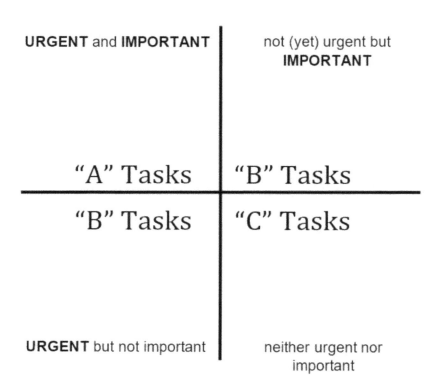

Figure 1.7 Sort your own tasks onto the priority grid.

How did it go? Was it challenging to figure out an "A" versus a "B" versus a "C" task? And, do you think you usually find yourself doing your "As" and "Bs" before you "Cs"? **Write down your thoughts about this activity here:**

_____

_____

Did you do the following?

- **Recognize some "C" tasks that might eat up time better spent on "A" or "B" tasks?** You might consider leaving some "C" tasks off of your list altogether. For example, buying a new video game might not need to be there because, if you forget, there are no dire consequences and you might be motivated to remember it regardless.
- **Look at your task list – especially those "A" tasks – and feel overwhelmed?** That's pretty normal when there's a lot to do but it's also good to recognize so you can be strategic with yourself. For example, you might occasionally prioritize an "easy" "B" or "C" task to maintain your motivation to tackle the task list. It may also be helpful to break down larger into steps that are easier to tackle.
- **Notice any tasks that are good candidates for "time cracks"?** If so, circle those and put them into your calendar on a day when there's a crack or two!

Nice work! To review, here's a summary of the ABC rating system:

"A" Tasks: urgent and important; MUST to be done today or tomorrow
"B" Tasks: less urgent but still important; some part needs to be done soon
"C" Tasks: lowest importance and urgency; these tasks are usually easy to do, so it's tempting to spend (waste?) time on them

---

Go for It!

Based on the practice you just did and the box here, **label each task on your task list with an "A", "B", or "C"**. With an electronic system, you can add a letter to the task item, color-code your items by priority, or make separate "A", "B", and "C" lists and move tasks between them as they change in priority. At least once per day, you'll need to add labels to new tasks and revise any labels on your existing tasks as deadlines approach.

Finally, you should commit to tackling those "A" Tasks, followed by some work on your "B" Tasks. But be patient with yourself! Learning this new system and being able to "work it" consistently will take time. You're going for consistent *practice*, not *perfection*.

- ☐ **Check here when you've finished labeling or listing your tasks by priority**
- ☐ **Check here when you're ready to commit to doing "A" Tasks <u>before</u> "B" Tasks before "C" Tasks.**

Module 1.4   Make Yourself Do Things

Even if you're using your calendar and task list system regularly and effectively prioritizing your tasks, you might still have trouble making yourself do certain tasks. All students struggle with motivation to do tasks at times, but for students with ADHD and executive functioning problems, difficulty motivating yourself can be a big barrier to getting things done. This module introduces several strategies that you can use to help you tackle the things on your task list.

Reward Yourself for Task Completion

Every living creature on the planet – including humans in general and college students specifically – is motivated to engage in activities that are followed by rewards, or what psychologists call *reinforcers*.

Sometimes though, students have a narrow view of what rewards are (think stickers or candy) or think they aren't "supposed to" need rewards to get themselves motivated. Instead, we encourage you to think flexibly and creatively about what rewards might motivate you and to fully embrace the use of self-reward to help keep you rolling in the right direction throughout the day.

Rather than thinking of rewards as things or objects, we prefer to think in terms of **rewarding activities** – for example, *eating* your lunch, *tasting* a caramel latte, *listening* to a podcast, *laughing* at an episode of The Office, or *seeing* the step count on your fitness tracker increase.

Jot down a few of your rewarding activities in the space given here. For example, **what would you do if you had a whole day free to yourself? What do you sometimes find yourself doing *instead of* items on your task list?**

_____   _____

_____   _____

_____   _____

_____   _____

Now that you've got a menu of rewarding activities, you're going to **pick one** and strategically **do it *after* you've completed a pesky task list task**.

We call this:

The When-Then Rule

For example,

- **When** I finish my chemistry homework, **then** I will watch an episode of *The Big Bang Theory*.
- **When** I have chosen a topic for my term paper, **then** I will play *Call of Duty* for 30 minutes.
- **When** I finish the first-page of my English paper, **then** I will get a coffee.
- **When** I finish washing the breakfast dishes, **then** I will eat lunch.
- **When** I finish reading this chapter, **then** I will tidy up my room (!)

Wait, what?! Tidying up your room may not *seem* like a particularly rewarding activity; however, we seem to remember suddenly getting VERY MOTIVATED to tidy our dorm rooms when we were supposed to be studying for finals! This is because the extent to which an activity is rewarding is both **personal** and **relative to other available activities**. So, it's important to consider what you personally find motivating and continue to add new activities to your menu. And, recognize that if a task list item like room-tidying is less icky for you than studying for finals, something like, "When I study for 30 minutes, then I can tidy up for 10 minutes", may in fact accomplish two items on your task list, using one as a reward for the other.

It's time to construct your first set of when-thens. Choose three (3) challenging tasks from your task list – maybe some A tasks or pieces of B tasks that need attention – and list them in the spaces under the **When** column. Next, identify a rewarding activity for each from the list you made earlier and put them in the **Then** column.

When I . . .   Then I will . . .

☐ _____   _____

☐ _____   _____

☐ _____   _____

Now, you need to figure out *when* exactly you'll carry out this plan.

☐ Check here when you've assigned these when-thens to a time in your calendar

---

 You should consider the *appropriateness* of different rewarding activities for various accomplishments. Choosing a term paper topic probably doesn't call for a large and potentially disruptive reward (e.g., watching a feature-length movie), whereas finishing your last take-home exam for the semester certainly could be followed with a major reward. Minor rewards that can be completed quickly, such as grabbing your favorite Starbucks drink, "surfing" your social media accounts for a few minutes (set a timer!), taking a quick walk, or calling a friend to catch up are great to use as short study breaks that also reward you for your efforts along the way.

Holding Yourself Accountable

When-thens are one strategy for helping to increase motivation. Here are a few other strategies for holding yourself accountable and increasing the likelihood that you'll follow through.

- pair up activities to create **rewarding routines**
- use **strategic scheduling** to maximize your motivation
- use **implementation intentions** to remember when to do things

First, creating **rewarding routines** can help you to tackle tasks that you might otherwise avoid. To do this, you'll **pair a difficult or unpleasant task with a more rewarding activity**. For example, suppose that you avoid doing laundry until you have almost no clean clothes to wear. You can establish a routine where you do laundry each Sunday evening <u>while</u> watching your favorite *Netflix* show or playing a favorite video game in between transferring and folding clothes. The strategy will be most powerful if you *only* watch that show or play that game during your weekly laundry time! By pairing the laundry with screen time, you may get the laundry done and find the process mildly enjoyable. And, in the long term, having clean clothes to start a new week will itself be a reward.

Try creating your first rewarding routine! First, choose **a task that you frequently avoid** and one that **you could possibly pair with another activity**. For example, don't choose reading assignments or writing because it's hard to do those at the same time as another activity or alternate between that and something else. Good choices might be chores, errands, organization tasks, or exercising.

Avoided Task:_____

Now, choose a rewarding activity that you will do – and ONLY do! – while you're engaged with the target task such as listening to a favorite podcast or playlist.

Rewarding Activity: _____

Finally, schedule this set of activities together in your calendar.

☐ Check here when your new rewarding routine is in your calendar.

Second, you can use **strategic scheduling** to optimize your productivity. For example, perhaps your big calculus class homework assignments are always due on Thursday mornings, but you have difficulty getting started on them until later Wednesday evening. If you schedule a weekly session with a tutor or study group on Wednesdays at 5 p.m., this can help motivate you to get started earlier than you would otherwise.

Take a look at your task list and **identify a task that you may have been avoiding** or one that you put off doing until the last possible moment. Next, **look at your calendar** for the next week and identify the time that you're most likely to be motivated to tackle that task. Could you pair it with another activity, such as your lunchtime? Could you use a "fun" activity that comes after it as a reward?

☐ **Check here when you've added the task to a strategic spot in your calendar**.

Third, you can boost the benefits of planning and strategic scheduling by stating or writing down an **implementation intention** – a statement about **when, where, and how you will do something.** Not only do implementation intentions help you make a plan to complete a task, but also imagining yourself doing the task in that situation can help you remember to actually do it. Here are some examples:

• After my psychology class on Monday morning, I will walk to the library, sit in the quiet study section, and study for one hour. (Imagine the walk from the psychology building to the library and then put the study time in your calendar.)
• When I brush my teeth in the morning (assuming you do this consistently!), I will take my ADHD medicine. (Imagine putting your toothbrush back in the holder and picking up your medication bottle. Maybe even duct tape your toothbrush TO the bottle!)
• When I go to the dining hall for lunch, I will call the student health service to schedule an appointment. (Imagine yourself going through the line, sitting at your usual spot, and taking out your phone before you take your first bite. Also, schedule the task on your phone and set a reminder.)

Positive Peer Pressure: Using the Help of Accountability Partners

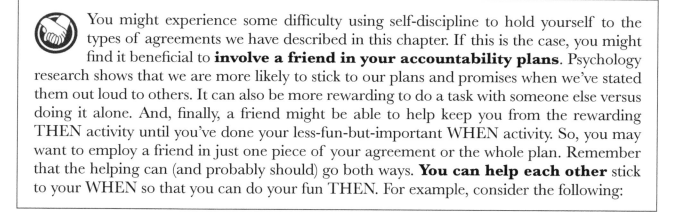 You might experience some difficulty using self-discipline to hold yourself to the types of agreements we have described in this chapter. If this is the case, you might find it beneficial to **involve a friend in your accountability plans**. Psychology research shows that we are more likely to stick to our plans and promises when we've stated them out loud to others. It can also be more rewarding to do a task with someone else versus doing it alone. And, finally, a friend might be able to help keep you from the rewarding THEN activity until you've done your less-fun-but-important WHEN activity. So, you may want to employ a friend in just one piece of your agreement or the whole plan. Remember that the helping can (and probably should) go both ways. **You can help each other** stick to your WHEN so that you can do your fun THEN. For example, consider the following:

- At the start of the day, tell your roommate the key thing you want to accomplish by the time you see them at the end of the day.
- Ask your roommate to do a 10-minute dorm room clean-up session with you before the two of you go get lunch together.
- Agree to play tennis or basketball with your friend only after each of you has finished your most important homework assignment for the following day.
- Ask your hallmate, who also wants to exercise more, to meet you at the gym on Wednesdays at 4:00 for bootcamp class. Then go to dinner together afterwards.

Who might make good accountability partners? **A good accountability partner is someone you're comfortable talking to about your goals and someone who will support (not sabotage!) you in meeting them.** Make a list of possible accountability partners in the space here:

_____

_____

Now take a look at your task list and choose a task you have been avoiding. It can be the same one you've picked for other strategies in this module! (Sometimes you need to super-charge your strategies to get things done.)

_____

Which person listed earlier might be a good partner for this task? Choose an aforementioned name and write out what your "ask" will be:

_____

_____

☐ Check here when you've texted or emailed your potential partner about your ask.

Go for It!

We've given you a LOT of possible strategies in this module to help make yourself do hard things. **The only way to know which will work for you is to try them out**! After you've tried some strategies, in the space here, write about **the results** of your experiments in accountability.

• **When-Then (Task Activity followed by Rewarding Activity):**

_____

• **Rewarding Routines (Pairing Task Activity with Rewarding Activity):**

_____

• **Strategic Scheduling:**

_____

• **Implementation Intention (Imagining exactly when/where you'll do a task):**

_____

• **Accountability Partner:**

_____

Module 1.5   Get Unstuck From Procrastination

Do you often put tasks off until the very last minute even when you *know* it's going to stress you out, mess up your sleep, and possibly have a negative impact on your grades or relationships? Many students, regardless of whether they have ADHD, struggle with **procrastination**. Procrastination can snowball: the more you procrastinate on tasks early in the semester, the more things start to pile up and you start to feel like you're constantly playing catch up on your work and maybe your sleep. On the flip side, procrastination can *feel good in the moment* because you can escape stressful thoughts and feelings and un-fun tasks, therefore increasing the likelihood of procrastinating again in the future. Overall, the downsides to procrastination generally outweigh any positives, so it can be very beneficial to learn strategies to decrease procrastination and increase motivation.

In this module, we cover three strategies for breaking the procrastination habit:

• **Break tasks down** into smaller steps
• **Notice and flip the scripts** (thoughts) you have about the task
• **Change the routines** preventing you from getting started

Break Tasks Down Into Smaller Steps

One reason for procrastination might be that the task is too large and overwhelming to tackle in one go. You might not know where to start and thinking about a task that big might just cause you to want to do anything BUT that task as soon as possible. For example, imagine that one of the tasks on your list is:

Write ten-page history paper.

How do you think you'd feel reading that item on your task list? Ready to jump right in to some historical research? Or, would you feel anxious, overwhelmed or just a sense of "UGH!" along with the urge to avoid? We think most students would feel the same way. Those feelings are a huge clue that this task needs to be broken down into smaller and less yucky steps. As a rule of thumb, if you don't know where to start, then the task is too big (Solanto, 2011). Or, put another way:

If you look at the task and want to RUN, then you need <u>smaller steps</u>!

Here's an example of how you could break down the task of writing the ten-page history paper:

1. re-read the directions for the assignment (always a good first step!)
2. choose a topic for the paper
3. find sources for the paper (literature search)
4. read and take notes on each source
5. create an outline for the paper
6. draft each paragraph (with a short break and small reward between each)
7. draft the introductory and concluding paragraphs
8. re-read and revise the paper for clarity
9. submit the paper to your professor.

We think that this list of steps provides a better "on ramp" to getting started because *re-read the directions for the assignment* is a smaller, more well-defined task that will set you off on the right path

Figure 1.8 Break big tasks down into smaller, more manageable steps.

for the rest of the task. And, as illustrated in Step 6, smaller tasks can be combined with small rewards (e.g., a when-then) per the strategies introduced in Module 1.4 to increase the likelihood of the steps being completed.

Breaking tasks down into smaller steps can also help you to figure out how to allocate your time in order to finish the task by the due date. If you determine that there are 12 steps involved in writing the paper and it is due in 14 days, you can set a goal for completing one step a day with two days allowed for breaks.

 Caution: Avoidance Ahead!

Sometimes students find that looking at the whole list of individual steps can be overwhelming because it lays out exactly how much needs to be done . . . which might be a lot. If this applies to you, **you can assign an A task rating to *just the next step*** and keep the full list of steps in the B section of your task list or in a separate space. One of the authors of this workbook does this by having a "Tasks for Today" section of her task list on Trello and moving the small pieces of a big task to that list as their turn comes up.

Okay, your turn. Choose a big task from your task list and follow the steps to break it down.

Task List Item: _____

What is the first, smallest step you can think of to get started on this task? (Hint: No step is too small.)

1. _____

Re-read that step. How badly do you want to run away? Make it smaller if you need to.

Next, draft a list of steps needed to complete the task. Don't worry if your list isn't perfect – this is a try-your-best *plan*, not a precise prediction of the future!

2. _____

3. _____

4. _____

5. _____

6. _____

7. _____

8. _____

(Add additional steps if you need to in the margins or on a separate piece of paper.)

Great! Look back at your steps. **Are there any places where you think you could add some when-thens, rewarding routines, or accountability partners to help you get things done?** If so, make notes about that on your list.

☐ Check here when you've added these steps to your task list and scheduled some time to work on putting the first step into your calendar.

Notice and Change Your Mental Script

A second powerful tool to get unstuck from procrastination is to first notice what you're thinking and feeling *just before* you procrastinate and then coaching yourself in a way that helps you engage rather than avoid. It makes sense, honestly, that students with ADHD might be particularly susceptible to unhelpful thinking about their ability to get things done, given that struggles with procrastination are so common. Examples of these types of thoughts include the following:

> *I can't do it.*
> *I can't pay attention right now.*
> *It's going to suck.*
> *I have more time to do it later.*
> *I'll feel like doing it later.*

Try this: Imagine it's time for the next step on the task list for the hypothetical ten-page history paper we talked about earlier. You're feeling a little tired already and you read the task list item:

Create an outline for the paper.

What **less-than-helpful thoughts** do you think you might have?

_____

_____

If you had some unhelpful thoughts that might veer you into Procrastination Territory, you're not alone. Research shows that students in general engage in this type of thinking and that students with ADHD are even more likely to have these procrastination-related thoughts. A further complication is that some adults with ADHD can, at times, be *overly optimistic* about their own abilities (including their ability to complete schoolwork) and about how long a task will take them to complete, which presents its own challenges to successful task completion (Knouse & Mitchell, 2015). And so the thoughts that push in the direction of procrastination aren't *always* negative ("I can't do it!") but often end up having negative consequences ("I can do it later!").

What can you do about this? The first step is simply to **start noticing your mental scripts** as they happen in those moments just before you avoid an important task. You might notice that the script is paired with a slight negative emotion, such as a twinge of anxiety, a sense of feeling hemmed in, or just an UGH kind of feeling.

The next step is to coach yourself differently. Don't try to suppress or push away the original less-than-helpful thought because research shows that doesn't work. Instead, **practice introducing new lines into your script**, such as:

Once I start, it won't be so bad.
I can do this for 30 minutes.
It'll feel great to finish this.
I can do hard things.
I'm being nice to the Me of the Future.

It's not easy to notice and change your scripts, so if you notice that scripts have a powerful effect on your procrastination, we recommend that you complete **Skillset 3: Thinking and Doing Differently**, which will give you much more in-depth practice with these thought-related skills.

How can you coach yourself to engage with a task rather than avoid? Write **some ideas for new scripts** here and then consider posting them by your desk, on your computer desktop, or at the top of your task list.

- _____

- _____

- _____

Change Your Procrastination Routines

Another reason for procrastination may involve becoming "stuck" in unhelpful routines that involve repeated patterns of thoughts, feelings, and actions. It could be beneficial for you to evaluate how your habits or routines are contributing to procrastination. Along these lines, a student might state that he "can't" study after 7 p.m. because his medication has worn off and he is "fried". Although working after 7 p.m. might be legitimately challenging, it's worth evaluating this routine to see whether there is more flexibility than meets the eye, since working after 7 p.m. might be necessary at certain times of the semester. This student's **unhelpful routine response** might go as follows:

1. Looks at next task list item: "Write ten-page history paper".
2. Feels tired and stressed. Notices that it's after 7 p.m.
3. *It's too late for me to start that now. I won't be able to pay attention at all anyway.*
4. Switches to playing video games "to relax".

Now, following this routine a couple of times probably won't result in too many negative consequences, but if the student repeats this routine until the night before the paper is due . . . well, it's probably not going to be a fun night.

In situations like this, how can you respond differently? Psychologist Russ Ramsay (2016) recommends developing **new routines** in procrastination danger zones. Steps can include:

1. Notice and acknowledge your feelings
2. Notice your mental script
3. Break down the task
4. Develop a WHEN-THEN for the first step
5. Coach yourself in a helpful way

For the student in the aforementioned example, this might look like:

1. **Notice and acknowledge your feelings:** *I'm feeling super tired and a little bit stressed. Lemme take a deep breath.*
2. **Notice your mental script:** *I notice I'm thinking that it's too late for me to start that now because I won't be able to pay attention at all. That's a thought I have a lot. But I also think I need to get a solid start on this paper and at least do a little bit.*
3. **Break down the task:** *Thinking about this whole ten-page paper is making me feel gross. It seems like I need to break it down, so how about I start by re-reading the assignment instructions and thinking about my topic.*
4. **WHEN-THEN for the first step:** *Then after I nail down my topic idea, I'll play Overwatch for 30 minutes.*
5. **Coach yourself:** *Good plan – go me! This won't be as bad as I thought.*

As usual, it's your turn! Try developing a new routine response for a situation that usually puts in you in Procrastination Quick Sand. You can think of ideas about a typical situation for you OR keep this page open in your workspace and go through the steps in an actual situation where you have the urge to avoid.

1. What are you feeling right now:

_____

2. What are you thinking? Is this script old or new? Helpful or unhelpful?

_____

3. What's a smaller piece of the next task you could do?

_____

4. How can you reward yourself for completing this step (WHEN-THEN)?

_____

5. What would a good coach say to you about this new plan?

_____

☐ Check here when you've completed this practice. You may want to copy down, print out, or post these steps in your workspace or on your computer to cue you the next time you feel the urge to procrastinate.

Go for It!

Congratulations for reaching the end of Skillset 1! You should now have a whole new toolkit for getting organized, managing your time, and completing tasks. Remember to continue to check and update your calendar and task lists on at least a daily basis, and to keep trying out the motivational techniques that were introduced in the last few modules.

At this point, it's good to take stock of which strategies seem to be the most useful and helpful for you so far. Take a moment to reflect here.

Module 1: Top 3 Most Helpful Strategies

1. _____

2. _____

3. _____

Module 1: Strategies I Still Need to Try Out or Troubleshoot More

1. _____

2. _____

3. _____

References

Knouse, L. E., & Mitchell, J. T. (2015). Incautiously optimistic: Positively valanced cognitive avoidance in adult ADHD. *Cognitive and Behavioral Practice, 22*(2), 192–202. https://doi.org/10.1016/j.cbpra.2014.06.003

Ramsay, J. R. (2016). "Turning intentions into actions": CBT for adult ADHD focused on implementation. *Clinical Case Studies, 15*(3), 179–197. https://doi.org/10.1177/1534650115611483

Safren, S.A., Sprich, S.E., Perlman, C.A., Otto, M. W. (2017). *Mastering your adult ADHD: A Cognitive-behavioral treatment program, client workbook.* Oxford University Press.

Solanto, M. V. (2011). *Cognitive-behavioral therapy for adult ADHD: Targeting executive dysfunction.* Guilford Press; /z-wcorg/.

2 Professional Learner Skills

Module 2.0   Why It Matters and Roadmap

For you as a college student, learning is a more-than-full-time job. You need to learn a huge amount of information quickly so that you can remember and use it when you need it most. You need to study and work for lengthy periods of time when all you really want to do is take a nap or hang out with friends. And you need to do all of this in an environment that seems tailor-made to distract you with other interesting activities and people. More than at any time in your life, the responsibility for learning falls squarely on your shoulders. The modules in this chapter are based on the science of learning and they're designed to give you specialized skills to learn more effectively and efficiently.

You've probably encountered "study skills" like these before. In the past, you may have gotten along just fine with the support you had in high school. Even when you've struggled, you may have thought, "There's nothing wrong with the way I study. 'Study skills' are just for people who need 'remedial help'". Yet, in our experience as college professors, we've found that the most successful students are those who are willing to experiment with and improve the way they do things, and this certainly includes those with ADHD. College can easily overwhelm the brightest of students because of the amount of learning and studying that needs to be completed across the semester. So we encourage you to keep an open mind about the skills in this module and be willing to try out some new strategies. Who knows? You may find your new *favorite* strategy in the pages that follow.

Check Yourself: Which Skills?

Complete the checklist to help you figure out which modules in this chapter may be most helpful for you.

DOI: 10.4324/9781003149620-3

Self-Assessment of Learning Skills. Complete the worksheet here, based on how these apply to you on a day-to-day basis in recent memory (about the last six months). Circle one response per item, using this scale: **0 = Never, 1 = Sometimes, 2 = Often, 3 = Very Often**.

1.	I get distracted when trying to study.	0	1	2	3
2.	It takes me a very long time to complete tasks and assignments.	0	1	2	3
3.	I have difficulty getting started on tasks I need to complete.	0	1	2	3
4.	I have difficulty sticking with tasks I need to complete.	0	1	2	3
5.	I avoid tasks that seem too big or overwhelming.	0	1	2	3
6.	I have difficulty remembering what I learned when it's time for the test.	0	1	2	3
7.	I complete my studying at the "last minute".	0	1	2	3
8.	I "cram" for tests and exams.	0	1	2	3
9.	I usually study by re-reading my notes or the textbook.	0	1	2	3
10.	I use flashcards but they don't seem to work for me.	0	1	2	3
11.	I have difficulty remembering what was covered in class or in readings.	0	1	2	3
12.	The notes I take in class are incomplete or unhelpful.	0	1	2	3
13.	I have difficulty asking my professors for what I need from them	0	1	2	3
14.	Professors don't seem to respond positively to my requests or emails	0	1	2	3
15.	I avoid using my peers as a resource for academic help when I need it	0	1	2	3

Make Your Plan

1. **Choose modules** based on the following and check them off in your plan here:

    Questions 1–5: If you marked several items "2" or "3", include **Module 2.1 and Module 2.2**.
    Questions 6–10: If you marked "2" or "3" for several of these items, include **Module 2.3**.
    Questions 11 and 12: If you marked either of these items "2" or "3", include **Module 2.4**.
    Questions 13–15: If you marked "2" or "3" for these items, include **Module 2.5**.

2. Look over the titles of the modules, in the following table, and flip through them briefly. **Include any additional modules that you think might be helpful** or that you're curious about.

3. **Work on the modules** you selected in the order that they appear by adding each module to your **task list and/or calendar** and tackling them one at a time. Check off each module when you finish it and **reward yourself for a job well done**!

Professional Learner Skills Plan

In my plan?	*Done*	*Module*	*Pages*
		Module 2.1. *Create Your Ideal Work Space*	**41–45**
		Module 2.2. *Get In (and Stay In) the Focus Zone*	**45–48**
		Module 2.3. *Power Studying*	**48–54**
		Module 2.4. *Take Effective Notes*	**54–57**
		Module 2.5. *Seek Help Effectively*	**57–62**

Module 2.1   Create Your Ideal Work Space

Like any professional, you as a professional learner need to have a space where you do your work. And, while it's hard to control the classroom environment, you can skillfully choose workplaces that will maximize your ability to learn and work efficiently when completing work on your own. In this module, you will set yourself up for success by thinking through exactly what you need to work and learn most efficiently. Staying on task during less-than-interesting work is a challenge under the best of circumstances. Yet it's been said that the best self-regulators simply put themselves in situations that don't require much self-regulation – they choose environments that help do the work of keeping them focused and on task. For example, choosing to write a paper in the same room where your friends are partying probably exceeds just about everyone's self-regulation ability. Even studying with your phone nearby or in bed when you're sleepy can be too much of a temptation. Why put that burden on yourself? This module is about lightening the self-regulation load, using the environment to boost your attention span.

 Check Your Motivation

Although it might be tempting to do your work "the old way" with your phone nearby or the TV on in the background, it's a good idea to consider whether these ways of doing things are in line with your goals. For example, maybe you'd rather get your work done so you can have more time to relax. Changing up your work space strategies might contribute to that goal.

Check Yourself: What Distracts You?

Complete the **first column only** of the following table with your own personal distractors. You can also ask a good friend or study partner what they've observed about you.

Source of Distraction	How to Manage
Sound/noise:	
Sights/visual:	
Comfort/discomfort:	
Devices:	
Other humans:	
Emotions:	
Thoughts:	

What keeps you "in the zone?"

Next, review the following list of distractions, based on what we've heard from students, and see if you want to **add anything to your personal list given earlier**.

Sound/noise: anything other than complete silence; complete silence distracts me; people talking, people whispering, music with lyrics; any music; noises that follow a rhythmic pattern (e.g., water dripping); and alerts coming from my phone/laptop

Sights/visual: phone/laptop notifications, TV screens, people in the room, lights that are too bright, and fluorescent lights

Comfort/Discomfort: uncomfortable seat, lack of writing surface, too hot/too cold, hungry, thirsty, and hung over

Devices: phone, laptop, TV, clock, specific apps, or websites

Other humans: friends, romantic partner or interest, and off-task people

Emotions: feeling confused, feeling tired, feeling anxious, and feeling sad

Thoughts: remembering something else I need to do; worry thoughts; thoughts about something I'd rather be doing

Now, think about things that have the opposite effect. In other words, what keeps you "in the zone", or focused on what you need to do?

What keeps you in the zone? Coffee, having taken my medication, feeling like I'm accomplishing goals, I need really (inspiring/chill) music, other people around me working and on task, making a checklist of small steps and ticking them off as I get things done

Management Strategies

Now, complete the **second column** of the table and think up some ways you could manage each distraction so that it doesn't derail you from the task at hand. Here are some examples to get you started:

Distracting noises: study in the silent section of the library; wear noise-canceling headphones; and listen to lyric-free music (e.g., film soundtracks).

Sights/visual: keep all screens (phone, TVs, and computer monitors) out of sight

Comfort/discomfort: make sure I'm warm enough; don't study in bed because I'll fall asleep; and study at a desk only

Devices: only study with devices completely turned off; remove apps that are key distractions; turn off app and email notifications on laptop; set a timer so I don't have to keep checking the clock

Other humans: study alone; study alongside a friend who's good at staying on task; study at a coffee shop or at the library where others are on task

Emotions: set a specific goal for the work period, read directions twice, do a short mindfulness/deep breathing exercise before getting started (see Skillset 3)

Thoughts: write a quick note to myself for later if I think of something I need to do, tell myself I can do a "rather be doing" thing later if I finish my work

Set Priorities

Looking back at your list, choose the TOP THREE (or slightly more or less) distractions you need to manage and list them here:

Distraction   How to Manage

_____   _____

_____   _____

_____   _____

_____   _____

Now, based on your priorities, choose an **ideal work location** and a back-up. Also, write down any strategies you identified for staying in the zone. Examples: silent study section of the library, cafe or coffee shop, smaller on-campus specialty library (e.g., law or music), less-used common room or other space in the dorms, outdoor locations, student workroom in your major department, desk in your room.

You can also ask other students about "secret study spaces" around campus.

Ideal Work Location

_____

Back-Up Work Location

_____

Strategies to Stay in the Zone

_____

_____

Now, when you have tasks to do that require maximum concentration, use the locations and the strategies you identified to set yourself up for success. Remember, you can always modify your plan if you learn new things about what works best for you.

 Stalling Tactics!

Sometimes your ideal study location isn't available or circumstances for doing work are less than ideal. Be careful that your ideal requirements for a work space on the previous page don't become excuses NOT to engage with a task. If you start spending excessive time making things just right for studying, you may be engaging in a stalling tactic! Use your back-up location or another "good enough" location.

Go for It!

The next time you settle in for a study or work session, first follow your new plan. To remind yourself, you may want to jot down some notes about this module in your task list or calendar.

☐ Check here when you've done that!

Module 2.2   Get In (and Stay In) the Focus Zone

There's no doubt that succeeding in college requires some long periods of sustained work and focus. From writing papers to doing computer coding to completing long reading assignments to reviewing for final exams, these tasks all require you to get "in the zone" and engage until the task is done. At the same time, these can be some of the most difficult tasks to get started on in the first place. Maybe you think to yourself, "UGH. This is going to take FOREVER", and instead do "just this one other thing first". Or, maybe you do get working for a couple of minutes and quickly find yourself checking your phone, talking to your roommate, or just spacing out without even realizing it. Either way, problems staying in the focus zone can contribute to procrastination, setting you up to be stressed out, sleepless, and behind on your tasks.

You're not alone. This module presents a set of strategies developed by a college student with similar struggles: The Pomodoro Method. When Italian university student Francesco Cirillo (2006) needed a way to keep himself on task, he found a game-changing tool in an unlikely place: his kitchen. Cirillo used a kitchen timer shaped like a tomato – *pomodoro* in Italian – to structure his work periods and resist distractions. It has helped thousands of college students (and professors!) to work and feel better.

Test Drive Time

The best way to learn any new skill is to try it out so let's jump right in. **You'll need about 30 minutes to complete this practice**.

• Think of a task you really need to be working on right now for school – something that's going to require some focus.
• Get access to the materials you need – that is, open up the reading assignment, open up the document file, or get set up otherwise. Open up a timer app on your computer or phone.
• Follow the four steps of the Pomodoro Method:

Step 1

What is your goal for *this work period*?

_____

Step 2

Set the timer app for 25 minutes[1] and work on the task. **Don't stop until the timer rings!**

☐ **Done**

Step 3

Set the timer for 5 minutes and take a *quick* break. Come back when the timer rings.

□ **Done**

Step 4

Next, you would start another Pomodoro. But for now, just keep reading.

Let's Assess

How did that go? Write down your thoughts about it here:

_____

_____

_____

Which of the following best describes your experience during the 25 minutes?

- □ I got into the zone on the task right away.
- □ It was hard to focus at first, but I fell into the zone before the timer rang.
- □ I struggled to focus the entire time and got a little distracted but I made it.
- □ I didn't make it the whole 25 minutes – I couldn't focus.

Any of these might have been true for you this time and they all are probably going to be true for you at one time or another using this strategy! **The more times you try, the more times you'll have the "zone experience".**

Which of the following best describes your experience when the timer rang?

- □ I didn't make it until the timer rang.
- □ I was so relieved I could stop!
- □ I was so in the zone that I didn't want to stop.

Again, any of these might have been true for you this time and they all are probably going to be true for you at one time or another using this strategy. **You can always skip a break if you really don't want to break your flow**, but remember to take a break when you get to a stopping point.

Which of the following best describes your experience with the break?

- □ I skipped the break and kept working.
- □ I took my 5 minutes and came back to the task.
- □ I took my break and got totally distracted.
- □ I never made it to the break.

You guessed it – any of these might have been true for you this time and they all are probably going to be true for you at one time or another. **If you have trouble keeping**

to a 5 minute break, you can think of some very specific tasks you'll allow yourself to do – like go to the bathroom, get a drink, or go outside and walk around the building and come back.

Pomodoro in the Real World

Nice work! To put this into practice in real life, instead of sitting down to work for a huge chunk of time, **you will divvy up your work periods into a string of pomodoros** (25-minute periods) with breaks in between.

Let's review the steps (Figure 2.1):

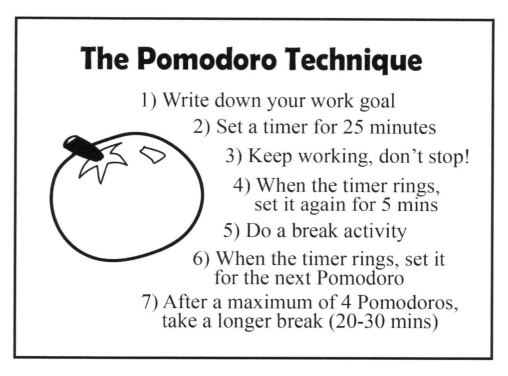

The Pomodoro Technique

1) Write down your work goal
2) Set a timer for 25 minutes
3) Keep working, don't stop!
4) When the timer rings, set it again for 5 mins
5) Do a break activity
6) When the timer rings, set it for the next Pomodoro
7) After a maximum of 4 Pomodoros, take a longer break (20-30 mins)

Figure 2.1 Summary of the pomodoro method.

 You *could* follow these steps all by yourself but – fortunately – **there's an app for that!** Lots of apps, actually, for smartphones and web browsers. Here are a few of our favorites.

- Pomodoro Timer Free or Pro
- Forest
- Focus Keeper
- Tomato Timer
- Focus To-Do

Go for It!

☐ **Check here** when you've downloaded a Pomodoro app from the app store

Choose a task from your list (such as writing or studying) that you will Pomodoro:

_____

☐ **Check here** when you've added this work session plan to your calendar.

Happy Focusing!

Module 2.3   Power Studying

Let's face it – you have lots to do and not a lot of time to spare. So what's the best way to learn and remember the **most** information with the **least** effort? Fortunately, the science of psychology has some pretty clear and useful answers. We refer to these strategies as **Power Studying** because, although doing them the first few times will feel a bit clunky, the results will be better memory, better grades, and less stress come test time.

Power studying involves three strategies:

* Study mostly by **testing yourself**
* Do it in **small chunks over time**
* Create **memory cues** for tricky information

We'll talk about these one at a time. But first, if you're up for it, let's do a demo.

Let's Learn Lithuanian!

Let's pretend you're taking a course to learn the Lithuanian language.

1) Set a timer for **2 minutes** and study the list of Lithuanian-English word pairs <u>in the following table</u> **only by re-reading them repeatedly** <u>to yourself</u>. **When time is up, cover the list up with a piece of paper**.

Lithuanian	English
pliažas	beach
nafta	oil
burna	mouth
mokykla	school
smegenys	brain
purvas	dirt
vejas	wind
tinklas	net
stogas	roof
pyragas	cake

<u>When time is up, cover the list up with a piece of paper</u> and don't look back at it!

2) Set the timer for **2 minutes** this time and study the new list of Lithuanian-English word pairs using any strategy you want. Again, cover the list up with a piece of paper when time is up.

Lithuanian	*English*
karalius	king
gele	flower
tiltas	bridge
sausainis	cookie
palaidine	shirt
batas	shoe
medis	tree
pastatas	building
ugnis	fire
durys	door

Cover the list up with a piece of paper when time is up.

3) QUIZ TIME! Fill in all the correct English words from the list you just saw (the second list) as you can remember.

Lithuanian	*English*
karalius	
gele	
tiltas	
sausainis	
palaidine	
batas	
medis	
pastatas	
ugnis	
durys	

Nice. We'll return to this later, but first:

Power Studying I: Self-Testing

You just studied those word pairs using two different methods: re-reading (or re-studying) and self-testing. Self-testing, according to hundreds of research studies, has been shown to be the more powerful strategy, no matter what you're trying to learn. One everyday example of self-testing is using **flashcards** – provided you put the prompts and answers on *opposite* sides of the cards AND you actually try to remember the answer before peeking!

Most students have a sense that using things like flashcards or the review questions in their textbook is a good idea, but research shows that a lot of students just fall back on repeatedly glancing over what they're trying to study versus doing the (slightly) harder work of self-testing. The problem, though, is that if you just read something, you're going to *think* you know it when you really don't. It seems counterintuitive, but **the harder you feel like you're working while studying, the more powerful the memory you're forming**.

So, we know that self-testing is the way to go and there are actually TONS of creative and interesting ways you might self-test. Remember:

<u>**Any time**</u> **you are trying to** <u>**pull information from memory**</u>**, you are self-testing**.

Here are more examples of what self-testing could look like:

Ideas for Self-Testing While Studying

- Use flashcard and quizzing apps (e.g., Quizlet)[2]
- Complete reading quiz questions at the end of textbook sections and chapters
- Draw important diagrams or concept maps from memory
- Write down everything you can remember about a concept or reading assignment
- Use the fold-over note page method (see next module)
- In a small study group, quiz each other on to-be-learned information
- Call your parent or grandparent and tell them what you learned in class that day
- Explain the main ideas of the reading assignment you just finished to your roommate

---

 Don't Drop Out!

Research studies have found that, when using flashcards, students typically "drop" a card from studying after they get it right just one time; however, dropping after **three (3) correct recalls** may be a better rule of thumb for powerful learning (Rawson & Dunlosky, 2011), and probably won't take you THAT much longer.

Power Studying 2: Anti-Cramming

So, you've probably heard this before: "cramming", waiting until the night before the test and studying all at once, maybe pulling an all-nighter – is bad. Why? First, lots of research in psychology shows that so-called "massed practice" (cramming) results in weaker memory than "distributed practice", such as studying in smaller chunks over time (Dunlosky et al., 2013). Also, when you cram, you're likely to be more highly stressed and/or sleep deprived – both conditions that are NOT good for your brain functioning and your memory.

But avoiding the need to cram is often easier said than done, and this is where your organization, time management, and planning skills are going to need to merge with your power studying. So, right now:

☐ Take out your calendar and identify a test or exam that's **more than a week away**.

☐ Go to the day that's one week before the test or exam and reserve some time, maybe 30–60 minutes, to study for the test on that day. Make sure to pick a time that's realistic – that is, not a time you tend to be sleepy or tempted to go out with friends.

☐ Next reserve about 3 additional time slots for studying. (approximately every other day)

☐ Reserve a larger slot the day before the test to put the finishing touches on your studying.

What are you going to do during those study sessions? You guessed it: SELF TEST in some way, which means that you're going to do what psychologists call "successive re-learning" or what we'll call "repeated re-learning". So, you're going to not only self-test on new information but also practice "old" information from prior sessions. The more times you can successfully self-test on information across sessions, the more powerful the memory. And when you get to that final pre-test study session, you should be working mostly on reviewing information you've already learned earlier in the week. Remember:

Repeated re-learning is using self-testing on the same material over time.

Hey, Remember Those Lithuanian Words?

Let's see if you really do! Without looking back, try to remember as many of the English translations as you can from each list you studied. **Skip the Number Correct slot for now**.

GROUP 1 (LIST S)

Lithuanian	English
pliažas	
nafta	
burna	
mokykla	
smegenys	
purvas	
vejas	
tinklas	
stogas	
pyragas	
List S – Number Correct	

GROUP 2 (LIST T)

Lithuanian	English
karalius	
gele	
tiltas	
sausainis	
palaidine	
batas	
medis	
pastatas	
ugnis	
durys	
List T – Number Correct	

Nice. **Now look back at the original list and grade your own paper. Write the number you got correct at the bottom of each column.**

So . . . What Was the Point of All That?

You may remember that we asked you to do two different things with those lists of word pairs. For List S, which stands for Study, we ask you just to re-read them. Over. And Over. For the other list, List T, we asked you to study them and then to try to recall as many as possible – **a self- Test**!

Looking at how many words you remembered from each list, did you:

- **Remember more words on list T than list S**: That *could* be because of the self-testing you did on List T versus the less powerful re-reading you did on List S.
- **Remember more words on list S than list T or remember the same from each list**: That's actually not too surprising. *The real power of self-testing shows over time.* Try coming back tomorrow or a few days from now and try the test again. See what you find!

Regardless of what came out in our little demo, at least you've gotten some practice with the strategy of self-testing *and* you've learned that spreading these self-tests over time is more powerful and, ultimately, less stressful.

In other words, you've learned the power of repeated re-learning.

Next, look back at the **Ideas for Self-Testing** on the previous pages and choose at least one new strategy you'll use to study for that upcoming test.

☐ **Make sure you've added each self-testing practice session to your calendar** before moving on.

Power Studying 3: Making Memory Cues

There's one more key component to Power Studying that comes from the science of how memory works: what psychologists call **mnemonics** or specific strategies that improve memory for certain kinds of information. Think of it this way – **memory works through connections.** We're better able to pull information out of memory if we connect it to other ideas that we already know and if we form interconnected networks of ideas. This process creates multiple **cues** that we can then use to pull the information out of memory. So, when learning certain types of information, you can create links to other types of information to aid your memory.

For example, **did you connect any ideas together** when you learned the Lithuanian-English word pairs? Write anything you did to learn and remember the items:

_____

_____

Maybe you used a phrase to link the two words, such as "That hot sauce sure did *burna* my mouth!" Or did you connect the Lithuanian word to something you already knew; for example, the Spanish word for beach (*playa*) reminding you of the Lithuanian *pliažas?* Or maybe you made up a crazy image in your head such as a building (*pastatas*) made entirely of pasta. All of these are examples of mnemonic strategies.

One tricky thing about using mnemonics is that certain strategies work better for certain kinds of information. Check out the descriptions in Table 2.1 and identify any mnemonics that might be useful for that upcoming test you're going to study for.

Making Memory Cues

Table 2.1 Mnemonic strategies and examples.

Type of Information	Method	Examples
Lists	**Acronyms:** words (or nonsense words) where each letter is a cue for a list item **Phrase mnemonics:** goofy phrases where the first letter of each word is a cue for a list item	**ROY G. BIV** = colors of the rainbow **PEMDAS** = mathematical order of operations **Every Good Boy Does Fine** (or Deserves Fudge) = ascending notes on the lines of treble clef musical staff **My Very Educated Mother Just Served Us Nine Pizzas**[3] = planets in order from the sun
	Method of Loci: you imagine a familiar path and then imagine placing objects along the path in order, using maximum visualization	You imagine your walk from your dorm to the dining hall, imagining each historical figure you intend to talk about in your speech standing at specific locations along the path.
Pairs of Items	**Visualization:** You imagine two or more items interacting in some way that produces a silly or otherwise memorable image.	To remember the names of her students, a professor visualizes each in a way that reminds her of their name – for example, Rob with a robber mask on, Miley running a mile
Rules of Thumb	**Rhyming phrases:** you learn a catchy poetic phrase to help you remember an important rule or other type of information	I before E Except after C Or when pronounced "ay" As in "neighbor" and "weigh" Thirty days hath September, etc.

Pull It Together

To wrap up this skill, do the following and check off each step:

☐ Choose an upcoming exam and add spaced study sessions for it to your calendar system
☐ Identify which self-testing strategies you'll use to learn the material for the exam
☐ Decide whether any mnemonic strategies can be helpful to learn that material
☐ Include notes about strategies in the calendar appointment to remind yourself

Happy studying!

Module 2.4   Take Effective Notes

From lengthy lectures to dense readings, students need to take notes to capture important information and have it handy for studying, writing, and thinking later on. Research has also shown that the act of note-taking can help students process information as they read or listen so that they can better remember it later. But the most important function of notes is that they act as a storage device and later as a study aid, letting you review the most important aspects of what you heard or read without having to listen or read all over again.

However, taking good notes can be a real challenge and maybe it's one you've struggled with. For example, some students have difficulty processing what's being said and getting it down on paper quickly and accurately. Other students have trouble identifying what's most important to include in their notes. Still others find that their notes are too disorganized to be useful when they come back to them later. In this module, you'll reflect on your own note-taking experiences and try out a straightforward but (potentially) helpful strategy.

Laptop or Longhand?

Taking notes on your laptop versus using pen and paper each have potential benefits and downsides. And you may decide to use these methods for different purposes – for example, using one method to take notes during lecture and another to take notes on readings. In the chart in Table 2.2, **circle the pros and cons that you think will apply most to you** and then use that information to consider where and when you might decide to use each note-taking tool.

Table 2.2 Pros and cons of note-taking styles.

	Laptop	*Longhand*
Pros	• Potentially faster than writing by hand, enabling you catch more information • Notes are searchable and easier to store	• Encourages summarizing or paraphrasing, which may aid memory • Presents less potential for distraction than laptop • Easy to add diagrams and drawings
Cons	• Presents a serious distraction temptation! • Slow typers may not benefit • Copying or typing verbatim may not aid memory much • Can be hard to add diagrams or drawings	• Potentially slower than typing, so might not catch as much • Storage and organization may be a challenge

A Tried-and-True Template

Okay, so how are you going to keep your notes organized? One well-loved method we recommend is **Two-Column Note-Taking** (Figure 2.2), based on the well-known Cornell Note-taking System.

1. Draw lines on your notes page to make it look like the following picture OR, if you're taking notes on your computer, search the internet for "notes template .doc" to find a Word file template.
2. As you read or listen, **write your notes in the large right column**. Use bullet points and abbreviations as much as possible so you can work quickly.

Title		Date
Main Idea	- more detailed notes	
Key Term	- detailed notes	
Key Term	- detailed notes	
Question?		
Main Idea	- detailed notes	
Summary		

Figure 2.2 Template for two-column note-taking.

3. **In the skinnier left column, write down main ideas, key words, and key questions** that *correspond* to the more detailed information in the big section. Things that might go in this column include:

   - Keywords from textbooks
   - Section headings or topic sentences from readings
   - Titles or main ideas from lecture slides
   - Key questions your professor asks during lecture
   - Anything your professor identifies as really important

4. Finally, **after you finish your note-taking for that section, write a few sentences of summary** of the information on each page at the bottom.

   Here's an example of how a student might use this method (Figure 2.3).

Ecology Notes	08/28/2022
Basic optimal patch use model	- foragers move through resource-containing patches separated by areas w/o resources - foragers should maximize net energy gain - a forager's energy intake rate goes down the longer it stays in the patch - it should stay in the patch as long as its current energy intake rate is higher than the expected rate elsewhere (time T)

Ideal free distribution model	- accounts for competition and predation
	- individuals should move to a lower quality patch if the per-capita energy intake rate is higher (b/c of less competition)
	- assumptions:
	  - consumers are equal competitiors
	  - consumers have perfect knowledge of resource availability
	  - consumers distribute themselves solely to maximize foragin efficiency

Calculating metapopulation occupancy	$dp/dt = cp(1 - p) - ep$
	  c = colonization rate per patch
	  e = extinction rate per patch
	  p = proportion of occupied patches
	- stable equilibrium for patch occupancy when $dp/dt = 0$

Summary	- foragers should maximize net energy intake - two main models for predicting foraging behavior - we can calculate patch occupancy

Figure 2.3 Example of two-column note-taking.

You can learn more about the Cornell Note-Taking System via this free, interactive online course! https://canvas.cornell.edu/courses/1451

Put Those Notes to Work

In the previous module, we told you about *repeated relearning*, a powerful strategy to maximally boost memory. Your two-column notes can be a great tool for testing yourself.

* Fold back the left hand column along the line you drew (longhand notes) OR cover the right column on your screen with another piece of paper
* Read each question or prompt in that column
* Try to remember everything you can from the reading or lecture about that topic
* Check your recall by turning over the page or revealing the answer on the screen

Above all, your notes can't benefit you if they're just sitting in your notebook or on your computer. **Studying notes actively and frequently will maximize their power**.

 Support System

Some students find that difficulties with *working memory* – holding information in mind while taking notes – or slower *processing speed*, which makes taking notes during lectures exceedingly difficult, even after trying the strategies we've recommended here. If that's the case for you, you may qualify for a *disability accommodation* in the classroom, such as getting permission to audio record your lectures. For more information on seeking academic accommodations, contact your college's disability services office or visit https://chadd.org/for-adults/legal-rights-in-higher-education-and-the-workplace/.

Module 2.5   Seek Help Effectively

College is not the time to "go it alone" when you find that you need help. A college campus is full of people whose full-time job is to provide different kinds of help and support to students. But different students can often find it tricky to seek help for different reasons. Do any of the following apply to you? Check any that seem familiar.

☐ I'm afraid to ask for help because I think it will make me look dumb or incompetent
☐ I think I can handle everything myself and then later realize I really did need help
☐ I put off asking for help until it's too late in the game to take advantage of it
☐ Sometimes I think I could use help but don't know what kind of help I need or who to ask
☐ I constantly have to email my professor to figure out what to do

From our experience with students, these are pretty typical challenges. Help-seeking isn't easy. You need to realize you need help, identify what kind of help you need, and then find the most effective way to get it. Fortunately, it's also true that **getting help is a skill that you can learn to do effectively**.

In this module, we'll cover:

* Using resources provided by your professors
* Using email to communicate effectively

- Collaborating with peers in your courses
- Getting help from campus offices and resources

Use Your Course Resources

Let's face it – not all professors are super-organized. But, in our experience, most instructors work hard to provide students with the information they need to successfully complete assignments and meet the course requirements. It's also our experience that students sometimes don't use these resources or forget that they exist. So, here is a list of potential ways to find answers to course-related questions. You may want to **jot these down on a sticky note and post the note** in your desk area or on your laptop.

Have a Question About Something in Class? Don't Wonder! Just Follow These Steps

- Carefully re-read any assignment instructions
- Check the syllabus for the answer
- Check the course's learning management system (e.g., Blackboard, Canvas, Moodle)
- Go to your instructor's office hours and ask your question
- If none of these answer your questions, email your professor or teaching assistant

---

Email Effectively

Do you ever dread opening your inbox because you fear you might drown in unread emails? Guess what – *your course instructors feel the same way*! So, to increase your chances of getting what you want from professors, you're going to up your email-writing game: That is, you're going to want to **write emails that get a positive reaction and that are easy for professors to respond to**. The first way to promote a positive response is to answer to this question:

What Should I Call My Professor?

Faculty members have worked hard to obtain their advanced degrees and, for many of us, it feels nice to be recognized for that work by being addressed with titles of respect such as "Dr." or "Professor". But, unfortunately, research has shown that *students are less likely to address professors who are women and/or people of color using these titles of respect*. So, when in doubt, **refer to your professor as Dr. _____ or Professor _____**. If they want you to call them something else, they'll let you know!

What Should I Say?

In short, clearly and concisely explain the situation and what you need from your professor. To guide you, we've developed the **DEAR PROF** method, summarized in Figure 2.4. You can take a picture of Figure 2.4 and make it your computer desktop background, post it to Instagram, etc.

Writing Effective Emails to Professors: Just Remember DEAR* PROF!

Describe: describe the current situation

> *"I was invited to interview for Teach for America; however, the interview is scheduled for the same day as our exam."*

Explain: explain your perspective on the situation

> *"I am concerned, since this is the only interview day and I will be unable to take the exam on the day it has been scheduled."*

Ask: clearly and specifically ask for what you want

> *"Therefore, I am wondering if you would please consider allowing me to take the exam two days early."*

Reward: explain positive consequences and "what's in it for them"

> *"I can be available to work around your schedule. Thank you, in advance, for your help."*

PROFessional: helpful subject line; address professor appropriately; greet and close

> *"Subject: taking the Intro Psychology exam early"*
> *"Dear Dr. Jones,"*
> *"Sincerely, Jon"*

Be sure to email a day or two **in advance** so that they have sufficient time to respond.

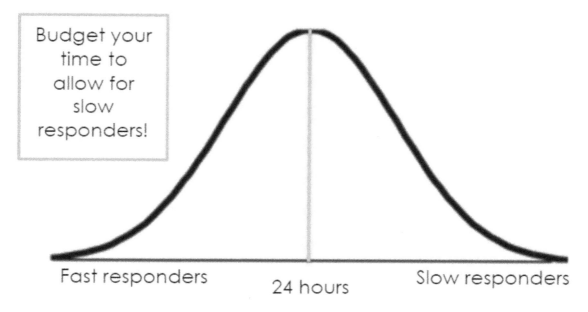

Figure 2.4 A strategy for emailing professors. *Adapted from DBT Skills Training Manual by Marsha Linehan (2014).

Start with a short and helpful subject line. It's nice if this also indicates the course and section you are in. Next, include four elements in your email. Each element can be short, but including all four ensures that your reader will understand the reason for your request and what exactly it is that you want. First, **Describe** the situation – just the facts. Next, **Explain** your perspective on the situation. In your view, what's the problem or concern? Next, clearly **Ask** the recipient what you want. If you're not sure what you want, you may be asking for advice about the situation, so just say that! Finally, indicate any **Reward** for the recipient (not for you!) for taking the time to consider your question (and help you, if possible). Many times, this can be just a simple "Thank You!" The figure gives a lengthier example, but for simple requests, DEAR can be pretty brief, such as:

Dear Dr. Flory,

I checked our syllabus and saw that the due date for our paper in Intro Psychology differs from what you announced in class yesterday. I want to make sure that I've got the correct information. Could you please clarify? Thank you so much!

Sincerely,
Laura Knouse

How Should I Say It?

Especially when sending your first email to someone, **it should probably read more like a letter than a text message**. Use a greeting ("Dear Dr. Knouse", "Hello Professor Canu!") and a closing ("Sincerely, Lauren, "Thanks so much, Donté") and write in complete sentences with capitalization, good grammar, and punctuation. From there, your recipient might respond more casually and then you can take your cues from that as you continue your conversation.

Be sure that you have appropriate expectations about response time. *You* might live on campus 24/7 and on weekends, but university faculty and staff do not. It's typically reasonable to expect a response within 24 hours (or so), Monday through Friday.

Finally, although it might not seem like a big deal, it's not usually a good idea to miss a class and then ask your professor, "Did I miss anything important?" It sounds like you're saying that their class might have consisted entirely of unimportant things!

Collaborate With Peers

In college and in life, your peers can be a crucial source of support. But your peers aren't just your friends – they also include your classmates, who may be willing to both give and receive help in order for everyone to succeed together. In this section, we outline three types of peer collaboration – getting class notes, studying together, and doing group projects – and offer tips for being effective in these relationships.

Getting Class Notes and Information

Classmates can be a great source of information if you happen to miss class. (Which you're only going to do *occasionally*, right?) While someone else's notes aren't ideal, they can be very helpful in filling in the gap created by a missed class and for getting crucial information about assignments that the profession might only share through class announcements. (Remember, you're typically responsible for information given in class even if you are absent.) Our three tips for effectively getting this kind of help are:

1. **Set it up early.** Identify a few classmates who could provide this kind of help in advance and ask them about it before you need it. Exchange contact information, if appropriate.
2. **Offer to reciprocate**. Let them know that you're happy to help them out when they need it and follow through on that commitment.
3. **Don't abuse it.** If you're calling on your classmate more than once or twice in the semester for their notes, you need to focus on strategies for getting to class more often.

Study Together

Collaborative studying can be a powerful learning tool . . . but it can also be a huge distraction. Here are three tips for effective collaborative study:

1. **Plan**. Before getting together to study, decide together what material you'll be studying and how you'll study it. Make sure the material to be covered is reasonable for the amount of time you have. Agree in advance that, if you get off topic, *anyone who brings the group back to the task at hand gets a big round of applause.*
2. **Choose a Space**. Make sure the space you choose to study is free from distractions, be that other non-studying students, your phones, or the TV. Group study rooms in the library, for example, can be a great choice.
3. **Test Each Other.** As we outlined in the Power Studying module, the best way to study is to work hard to remember the information you're trying to learn. Take advantage of peer studying by quizzing each other or summarizing and explaining information to each other.

Group Projects

Ah, the dreaded group project! Everyone probably has a heinous group project story; however, learning to work collaboratively is such an important professional and life skill that it's part of the learning outcomes for many college classes. Here are three tips for being a great group project member:

1. **Communicate Often.** Respond quickly and clearly to communications from your group members. Even if you don't know the answer to something, let them know you are listening and staying engaged.
2. **Make a Plan.** Encourage your group to establish a clear plan for each group member at the end of each meeting. Each member should know what they are supposed to do and when they are supposed to complete the work. If you find you can't do what you say you'd do, see #1.
3. **Don't Avoid.** Whatever you do, don't "check out" of the group. Stay engaged, even if group members disagree. If you're having conflict with another group member, ask to speak

with them about it one on one rather than letting it fester and get worse. If your group runs into major interpersonal issues, speak with your course instructor for advice in navigating the situation.

Use Campus Offices and Resources

Professors and peers are most definitely NOT the only people on campus who can help you succeed in your classes. Most campuses have a whole list of campus support offices and staff to provide help for students in specific areas. You might have only heard about these offices during orientation and, by now, you may have completely forgotten that they exist, so we're reminding you.

Could you benefit from any of the following types of help? Even if not right now, your assignment is to learn more about what one of these offices has to offer. **Check off the one that seems most useful** and make a plan to reach out!

☐ Individual or group tutoring in a specific course (Academic Skills Center)
☐ Coaching on how to better manage time and study (Academic Skills Center)
☐ Planning for and feedback on a paper you have to write (Writing Center)
☐ Planning for and feedback on a presentation you have to give (Speech Center)
☐ Help finding sources for a research paper (Librarians or Reference desk)
☐ Classroom accommodations and support for a disability (Disability Services)
☐ Therapy or medications to help you better manage your ADHD in college (Counseling Center or Student Health Center)

For any sources of help you checked next, **look up the contact information for that office** and jot it down here (if it's an online form, go ahead and fill that out):

_____

Finally, **contact the office and set up an appointment** to learn more about their services.

☐ Check here when you've done that.

Happy Help-Seeking!

Notes

1 In this approach, 25 minutes is referred to as a pomodoro (a unit of time).
2 You may be able to find pre-made sets of flashcards or questions on Quizlet associated with their textbook or on the textbook publisher's website.
3 Yes. We are aware that Pluto is no longer officially a planet, but we think that was pretty harsh. Take that, International Astronomical Union!

References

Cirillo, F. (2006). *The Pomodoro Technique.* http://friend.ucsd.edu/reasonableexpectations/downloads/Cirillo%20-%20Pomodoro%20Technique.pdf

Dunlosky, J., Rawson, K. A., Marsh, E. J., Nathan, M. J., & Willingham, D. T. (2013). Improving students' learning with effective learning techniques: Promising directions from cognitive and educational psychology. *Psychological Science in the Public Interest, 14*(1), 4–58. https://doi.org/10.1177/1529100612453266

Linehan, M. M. (2014). *DBT skills training manual* (2nd ed.). Guilford Press.

Rawson, K. A., & Dunlosky, J. (2011). Optimizing schedules of retrieval practice for durable and efficient learning: How much is enough? *Journal of Experimental Psychology: General, 140*(3), 283–302. https://doi.org/10.1037/a0023956

3 Thinking (and Doing) Differently

Module 3.0   Why It Matters and Roadmap

Sometimes, even when you know what you *should* do and you know *how to do it*, you can find yourself falling back into old patterns. Maybe that's been the case with some of the things you've learned so far in this workbook. For example, you might "know" it's a good idea to write everything down in your planner or task list, but sometimes you think, "I don't need to do that *this* time". Or maybe a setback makes you think, "These self-testing strategies don't really work for me. Why even bother?" Either way, sometimes your thoughts and feelings can derail you from using the skills that help you cope with your ADHD symptoms. That's what this chapter is all about – learning how to recognize and roll with thoughts and emotions so that you can act in the way that's the kindest to the *You of the Future*.

Check Yourself: Which Skills?

Complete the checklist to help you figure out which modules in this chapter may be most helpful for you. Note that, in this skillset, we recommend that everyone complete Modules 3.2 and 3.3.

Complete the following worksheet, based on how these apply to you on a day-to-day basis in recent memory (about the last six months). Circle one response per item, using this scale:[1] **0 = Never, 1 = Sometimes, 2 = Often, 3 = Very Often**.

1. I could be experiencing some emotion and not be conscious of it until sometime later.   0 1 2 3

2. I find it difficult to stay focused on what's happening in the present.   0 1 2 3

3. I don't notice feelings of physical tension or discomfort until they really grab my attention.   0 1 2 3

4. It seems I am "running on automatic", without much awareness of what I'm doing.   0 1 2 3

DOI: 10.4324/9781003149620-4

5. I could be experiencing certain thoughts and not be aware of them until later.	0 1 2 3	

6. When I feel bad, I do things I later regret in order to make myself feel better now. 0 1 2 3

7. When I am upset I often act without thinking. 0 1 2 3

8. I tend to lose control when I am in a great mood. 0 1 2 3

9. It is hard for me to resist acting on my feelings. 0 1 2 3

Make Your Plan

1. **We recommend that you include Modules 3.2 and 3.3 in your plan.** These represent **central** skills for well-being and success in college and in life in general.
2. **Choose additional modules** based on the following and check them off in your plan:

> Questions 1–5: If you marked several items "2" or "3", include **Module 3.1**.
> Questions 6–9: If you marked "2" or "3" for several of these, include **Module 3.4**.

3. **Look over the titles of the modules** in the following table, and flip through them briefly. Include any additional modules that you think might be helpful or that you're curious about.
4. **Work on the modules** you selected in the order that they appear by adding each module to your **task list and/or calendar** and tackling them one at a time. Check off each module when you finish it and **reward yourself for a job well done**!

Thinking and Doing Skills Plan

In my plan?	Done	Module	Pages
		Module 3.1 *Mindfulness: Becoming Aware*	**65–72**
Yes		Module 3.2 *Notice Your Patterns*	**72–76**
Yes		Module 3.3 *Practice New Responses*	**77–82**
		Module 3.4 *New Responses II: Impulsive Emotions*	**82–86**

Module 3.1   Mindfulness: Becoming Aware

If you think about it, I bet that you can identify many things that you do in life that happen pretty much automatically, or, in other words, like you are on auto-pilot. Take, for instance, driving a long distance on the highway. While you're going through all the motions of driving – keeping yourself in your lane and passing when you need to, setting and keeping your desired speed, and maintaining appropriate distance between you and other cars – you may lose awareness of doing these things, and maybe even of the vehicles that are keeping pace around you. You get lost in your thoughts or maybe in a podcast or music, and may even arrive at your destination or exit and suddenly jerk back to awareness, wondering how you got there successfully. This can happen in everyday life, too, like when you start to brush your teeth and don't really think about it until you have done your two minutes, or finding that you can completely unload your groceries while only really paying attention to your roommate who is chatting at you.

Why are we bringing this up? What do these things have to do with *thinking differently*? The answer is that they have to do with **mindfulness**, or, actually, the lack of it. Mindfulness is *purposefully paying attention to the present moment*. Mindfulness is important to everyone, and maybe especially to college students with ADHD, because it keeps us rooted in what is happening *in the now* and can help us figure out *what works and what doesn't*. Mindfulness is a skill that involves being able to direct your attention to the thing that needs it most or that you want to focus on and the ability to not have your attention "pulled away" by unhelpful things.

Another important aspect of mindfulness is a *non-judgmental attitude* toward the things you're paying attention to – especially the thoughts, feelings, and actions that you become aware of through mindfulness. This means being able to slip more into an "observer" role instead of an "evaluator" role – that is, to notice what is happening without judging it or reacting to it emotionally. For example, a non-judgmental attitude allows you to notice what's happening in your environment (e.g., it feels hot, you can hear cars outside) and what's happening inside of you (e.g., the thought "I really want to go home", a feeling of stress), without getting too wrapped up in it and then being able to shift your attention to other things.

Given what you already know about ADHD, you probably are getting the picture of how mindfulness can be especially difficult for people with ADHD. Challenges central to ADHD, like inattention, emotional dysregulation, and executive functioning problems, can make it difficult to stay mindful. And while you don't need to be mindful *all of the time*, there are many instances in which mindfulness is critical to success and well-being. For example, you could be at a party and really want to listen to and connect with the people around you, but your attention might be so wrapped up in the nervous thoughts and feelings you're having that you can't pay attention to really "be there". Or, take the example of highway driving, one from one of our own personal experiences. You could be driving down the highway, in that unmindful zone, not really noticing things around you much . . . and fail to notice THE CAR COMING RIGHT AT YOU in your own lane!!!

Your turn! What are some other examples of activities where lack of mindfulness is a problem?

_____

_____

_____

Are there any settings or activities where you actually have good mindfulness?

_____

_____

_____

Fortunately for Dr. Canu, in the driving situation, mindfulness kicked in, just in time . . . he got out of the way of that car and lived to tell the tale. But this is a good analogy for lots of situations that you might face, like a big term paper, assigned at the beginning of the term. You may be "driving along", doing daily work and studying for tests and quizzes, but missing awareness of the term paper until BAM!!! It's midnight and your friend in the class texts you saying how good it is to be done with the paper, which is due the next day . . . and you are out of time and energy to pull it together. So mindfulness can help us to expand our awareness and to see all the things that are potentially worthy of our attention.

Mindfulness can also really help with *thinking differently* when unhelpful thinking crops up. That *non-judgmental* stance really comes in handy here. Let's say that you have not completely forgotten about your term paper, but it's due in a couple of days and it's been hard to get down to the business of getting it done. Negative thinking might creep in here, like "I can't believe how hard this is for me! I am so lazy and I'll never get this done!" Thoughts like that can have a lot of power . . . you might get stuck on them, and if they dominate your awareness, that's unlikely to help you get the paper finished. Practicing mindfulness could help you "see" that thought, acknowledge that it is a thought of yours, and then let the thought go . . . and, potentially open yourself to awareness of thoughts like, "Hey, I remember that workbook said that if I'm procrastinating, I should break down the task and use a WHEN-THEN as a reward" (see Module 1.5). You're not just saying to yourself "It's no big deal". Instead, you're acknowledging the difficult things and making space to see the neutral, helpful, or even downright positive things that are present in the moment, too.

Understanding Check!

In your own words, what is mindfulness?

_____

_____

_____

How Mindful Am I? Could It Help to Be More Mindful?

Like with most things, there's a really wide range of mindfulness abilities across people. Where you fall on this spectrum can be due to natural inclination but it's also influenced by experience and practice – it's a skill you can learn. Zen Buddhism is a spiritual orientation that cultivates mindfulness, especially through meditation. Perhaps this is something you're familiar with and, if so, it may have helped you to develop mindfulness. Some kinds of therapy also include mindful practice, and maybe that's something you have encountered, too. Wherever your life path has taken you and whatever your natural tendency toward mindfulness, we believe that **it is always possible and beneficial to cultivate mindfulness skills**.

As mentioned earlier, mindfulness often doesn't come easy to people with ADHD. A few research studies have focused on training children and adults with ADHD in mindfulness skills, and while the overall outcomes for reducing ADHD symptoms have been relatively modest (compared to cognitive-behavioral or medication therapies), participants in those studies reported high satisfaction. In other words, developing mindfulness may be something that you experience as positive, in various ways.

To get a sense of your mindfulness starting point, complete the following questionnaire (Lau et al., 2006), and score it given the instructions that follow.

Please read each statement and the extent to which you agree. In other words, how well does the statement describe your experience?

	Not at all	A little	Moderately	Quite a bit	Very much
I experience myself as separate from my changing thoughts and feelings.	1	2	3	4	5
I am more concerned with being open to my experiences than controlling or changing them.	1	2	3	4	5
I am curious about what I might learn about myself by taking notice of how I react to certain thoughts, feelings or sensations.	1	2	3	4	5
I experience my thoughts more as events in my mind than as a necessarily accurate reflection of the way things "really" are.	1	2	3	4	5
I am curious to see what my mind is up to from moment to moment.	1	2	3	4	5
I am curious about each of my thoughts and feelings as they occur.	1	2	3	4	5
I am receptive to observing unpleasant thoughts and feelings without interfering with them.	1	2	3	4	5
I am more invested in just watching my experiences as they arise, than in figuring out what they could mean.	1	2	3	4	5
I approach each experience by trying to accept it, no matter whether it is pleasant or unpleasant.	1	2	3	4	5
I remain curious about the nature of each experience as it arises.	1	2	3	4	5
I am aware of my thoughts and feelings without overidentifying with them.	1	2	3	4	5

	Not at all	A little	Moderately	Quite a bit	Very much
I am curious about my reactions to things.	1	2	3	4	5
I am curious about what I might learn about myself by just taking notice of what my attention gets drawn to.	1	2	3	4	5
Total Score =					

Focus on your total score. In a group of non-ADHD adults, the average total score for current mindfulness was *approximately 29*, and an estimate of "average range" for scores is 20–38 (Klein et al., 2015). Total scores lower than 20 could be thought of as "lower" mindfulness and above 39 could be considered "higher" mindfulness. Where did you fall?

Practice Mindfulness

Like most things in life and in this workbook, getting better at mindfulness is something that takes intention and practice. The first step is to realize that, in many moments of our lives, we are really not very mindful at all.

So, a good first step in being more mindful is actively paying attention to your experiences. Basically, you're going to repeatedly practice noticing all of the things that are going on *right now* in the environment and inside of you. Like with any skill or ability, mindfulness gets better with practice, and this is a way to do it in your "real life". **Check out the form on the next page you can use to guide your noticing practice.** You'll see it asks you to notice what's coming in via your five senses, what you feel inside your body, and what kinds of movements and thoughts are happening.

Spend a few minutes noticing and record your experiences in the first blank row of the form RIGHT NOW and then come back here for the next step. (We'll wait.)

Good work! Did you notice there were more potential things to be aware of than you thought there'd be? It's sort of amazing what our brains are filtering out at any given moment.

Over the next day or so, you're going to do some noticing practice several more times. It's not super important exactly when you choose to do your practice – the idea is just to experience purposefully noticing *more than you usually do*.

When would be the best times each day to do this? Try setting some alarms in your phone for a few random times over the next couple of days. Also, you'll want to put this practice in your calendar to remind yourself.

☐ Check here when you've put this practice on your task list or in your calendar and set some reminders.

Practice Noticing

Instructions: In several different moments over the next few days, notice what is going on in the environment and inside of you and record it in the following table.

What do I SEE?	What do I HEAR?	What do I SMELL/TASTE?	What do I feel ON MY SKIN?	What do I feel INSIDE MY BODY?	How is my body MOVING?	What THOUGHTS do I have?
EXAMPLE: The dim light of my desk lamp and the bright light of my laptop screen. Darkness in the room around me.	My roommate snoring softly; the air conditioning blowing; muffled music from the room next door	Slight bitter taste from the coffee I just drank. Scent of the lotion I put on my hands.	Slight coolness from the lotion. The pressure of the chair on my rear end. My feet resting on the floor.	Slight pain on the sides of my head. My breath going in and out. The urge to tap my left foot.	Still except for blinking and the movement of my chest up and down as my breath moves. Hand moving to write all this down.	This is a LOT of stuff to write down. Is this really going to help me? I feel really tired right now. I'm almost done, thank goodness.

What Can I Do to Develop Mindfulness Further?

You can use various exercises to help you develop your mindfulness ability further. Which of the following options appeals to you most? **Check it off and then look at the information on finding resources for practice**.

☐ Follow **guided meditations** you can find online or through an app
☐ Engage in **activities** mindfully, such as walking or eating
☐ Try a **mindfulness-oriented group practice**, such as yoga or group meditation
☐ Check out **books or websites that provide instruction in mindfulness practice**, some tailored to ADHD.

Apps (Android/iOS) and Online Guided Meditations

Headspace
Calm
UCLA Mindfulness (free)
Mindfulnessexercises.com (free)

Activities

Mindful eating: Take a grape (or raisin, or chocolate chip, or a berry) and, before and as you slowly eat it, focus on this with all of your senses: sight, touch, smell, taste, and sound. Notice what else happens in your body, and your thoughts and feelings. If your attention wanders from these experiences, notice that, and gently, nonjudgmentally, turn your focus back to the grape (or other morsel).

Mindful walking: Starting from a seated position, stand up and walk to a destination that will take five or so minutes. Notice sensations in your body, and try to keep your attention there. What do you sense in your muscles, your breathing, and your heart? As you walk, how does the air feel? Do you hear, smell, or see things as you walk? Notice and acknowledge these sensations as well as any thoughts or feelings that come, but shift your focus back to your body, nonjudgmentally, as you complete your walk.

Mindfulness-Oriented Group Practice

Yoga – Many types of yoga involve a blend of physical movement and mindfulness practice. Your college's recreation center may offer yoga or mindfulness to you for free. Fitness apps like Glo Yoga or the Peloton app also offer yoga and meditation options although paid subscriptions are often required. Luckily, though, some generous instructors offer recorded yoga classes for free on YouTube.

Group Meditation – Group meditation sessions may be offered on your campus through the student health and recreation center or coordinated by faculty, staff, or students interested in regular mindfulness practice. Community groups, including some religious organizations, may offer meditation sessions as well but if you're not comfortable with the religious aspects of meditation, you should choose other mindfulness practice options mentioned earlier.

Books (May Be Available in Audiobook or Kindle Formats, Provide Lots of Great Info)

Zylowska, Lidia (2012). *The Mindfulness Prescription for Adult ADHD*. Trumpeter Books.

Kabat-Zinn, Jon (2012). *Mindfulness for Beginners*. Sounds True Publishing.

Shapiro, Shauna, & Siegel, Daniel (2020). *Good Morning, I Love You: Mindfulness and Self-Compassion Practices to Rewire Your Brain for Calm, Clarity, and Joy*. Sounds True Publishing.

Websites

Mindful: Happy Mind, Happy Life. www.mindful.org

Oxford Mindfulness Centre. Pay-per-course but also has free resources that are very helpful at www.oxfordmindfulness.org/learn-mindfulness/resources/

Tasting Mindfulness. Blog by Lynn Rossy, Ph.D., a health psychologist focusing on mindful eating, moving, and living. Lots of interesting content. www.lynnrossy.com/tasting-mindfulness/

Which resource are you going to try and when will you use it in the next week? It's also okay to keep using something that's already working well for you. Make some notes here:

_____

_____

☐ Check here when you've put this practice on your task list and in your calendar and set a reminder.

Next Steps

When you have practiced mindfulness and self-monitoring for a week or so, you should be ready to move on to the next module. Take what works for you, and make it part of your routine!

Module 3.2   Notice Your Patterns

A good first step to making any change is to get some information about the *status quo* – the way things are. In this module, you'll get curious about how your thoughts, feelings, and behaviors all influence one another and how these patterns can contribute to struggle or success working with your ADHD.

Wait, Do Thoughts and Feelings Cause ADHD?

Short answer: no. ADHD symptoms are primarily caused by neurobiological factors related to genetics. However, there's substantial (and growing) evidence that the thoughts you have and the way you feel in response to those thoughts can influence how well you cope with your ADHD. On the flip side, the actions you take to try to cope with ADHD can also affect how you feel about yourself and what you think you're capable of in the future. Thoughts, feelings, and behaviors are all connected in a big, interactive circle. It's complicated, but, on the good side, it means that you've got lots of different "entry points" to making things work better. That's what the remaining modules in this skillset are about.

We have developed a model for understanding how thoughts – or *cognitions* – can interact with ADHD symptoms to influence how well a person can cope and how much ADHD symptoms cause problems. Take a look at the picture in Figure 3.1, and we'll explain more:

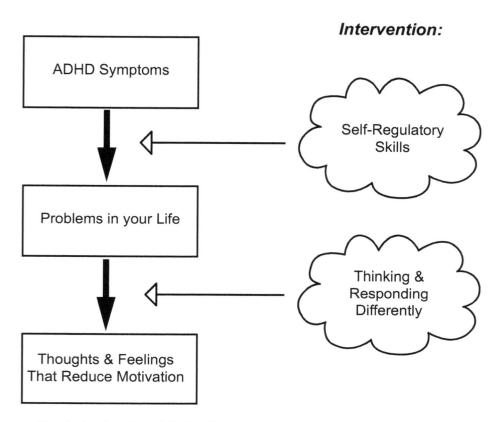

Figure 3.1 A cognitive-behavioral model of ADHD.

- ADHD symptoms contribute to problems in your daily life – *but* using the self-regulation skills covered earlier in this workbook can help to reduce those problems. Skills won't get rid of your symptoms, but they can help you work around them and make them less problematic.
- For some people, the problems caused by ADHD affect the way they think and feel about themselves and their ability to meet goals.

Has living with ADHD affected the way you think and feel about yourself and your ability to change? If so, how?

_____

_____

_____

- When these thoughts and feelings show up in daily life, they can make it harder for you to commit to and follow through on actions that could make things better – in other words, they reduce your *motivation*.
- And, when de-motivating thoughts and feelings are dominating your head space, they can also make it more difficult to use the skills in this book. So, addressing these patterns of thoughts and feelings can clear the way to making better use of skills.

So, the Next Step Is to. . .

1) **NOTICE** thoughts and feelings that reduce motivation, and
2) **RESPOND** with more helpful thoughts and actions

Like all the new skills in this book, this one's going to take some practice so let's get started.

A Map for Your Patterns

To get better at noticing your patterns, it can be helpful to have a framework to help you recognize them. We've talked about how thoughts (cognitions), feelings (emotions), and behavior (actions) all influence one another and, sometimes, not in a helpful way. See the following diagram (Figure 3.2) for an example pattern for a student we'll call Alex.

Alex is working on their time management skills and sets the goal of using their Google Calendar daily. For the past five days, it has been going well. But then they forgot to put a meeting with their research advisor into their calendar and no-showed this important appointment. When reflecting on what they felt, what they thought, and what they did next with the planner, Alex wrote down the following (Figure 3.2):

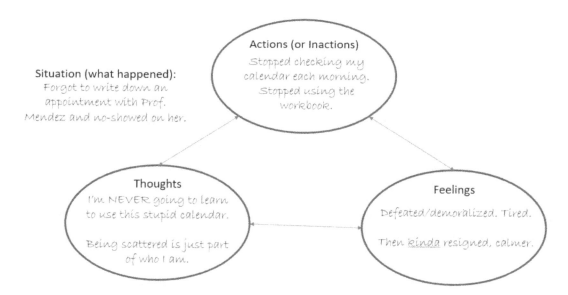

Figure 3.2 Alex's thought–feeling–behavior pattern.

Alex (understandably!) felt bad about missing the appointment and they also saw the situation through a particular cognitive lens. According to Alex's thoughts, missing the appointment wasn't just a mistake – their thoughts about the situation turned that mistake into a sign that Alex would *never* be able to learn the skill and, even further, that they're stuck being the way they are with no possibility of growth. From the perspective of Alex's current way of thinking, it makes sense (in a way) that Alex isn't terribly motivated to keep trying with the Google Calendar or with their new skills at all. But if Alex decides *not* to try again, they may have missed the chance to learn helpful skills that could ultimately help them avoid missing future meetings with people important to them. And we know it might seem cliché, but we've seen it over and over: making mistakes while learning new skills is an *expected* and sometimes even *necessary* part of the process of gaining new skills.

Now it's your turn to map a pattern. Think back to a specific situation in the past week or two where you have experienced problems that are related to your ADHD symptoms and fill in the diagram (Figure 3.3). If you can't think of an ADHD-related example, try to zero in on a time when you experienced a difficult emotional response and try to remember and recount the situation, your thoughts, and what you did in response (Figure 3.3).

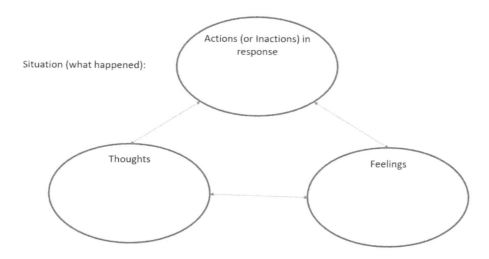

Figure 3.3 Your thought–feeling–behavior pattern.

What did you notice about what you wrote? Do your thoughts, feelings, and actions in response seem to relate to one another? If so, how?

_____

_____

_____

_____

Practice Identifying Your Patterns

Becoming aware of patterns in daily life takes practice, so that's what we're going to ask you to do. Using the sheet on the next page, **at least once per day for a few days**, fill in information about a situation and thoughts, feelings, and actions in response. Ideally, these should be events that you think are related to your ADHD, but they can generally be things that happened that you felt were difficult or stressful.

Ask yourself now: When would be the best time each day to do this? Then, put this practice in your calendar to make sure it gets done over the next week.

☐ Check here when you've put this practice on your task list or in your calendar and set a reminder.

When you've collected a few real-life examples, it's time to move on to the next module.

Happy Noticing!

Noticing Your Patterns

Instructions: For at least one situation per day, complete the following table. Choose situations where your ADHD symptoms contributed to problems for you. Alternatively, you can choose situations where you experienced strong emotions.

Situation – when and where?	Feelings	Thoughts	Action	Why was this action problematic?
EXAMPLE: In my dorm room; 10 p.m. on Sunday. Paper due tomorrow at 5 p.m. and I've been putting it off for hours	guilty UGH! overwhelmed	I don't want to do this! I should have started hours ago. This is going to suck. I need to have this desk clean before I can get started.	Spent 45 min. organizing my desk	I needed to be working on my paper. Organizing the desk ended up making me feel worse in the long run.

Module 3.3   Practice New Responses

In this module, we'll build on your observations from the prior module to begin to create and practice new and more helpful ways of responding in challenging situations.

What Did You Notice?

Look back at the *Noticing Your Patterns* sheet from the past few days. Take a few minutes (maybe set a timer?) to think about what you observed and write those observations here. In particular, **write about any times when thoughts impacted your motivation to take action, use skills, or address a problem in the most effective way**.

_____

_____

_____

_____

_____

_____

_____

_____

_____

_____

Nice. We'll come back to these observations throughout the work we do in this module.

How Are You Coaching Yourself?

In a way, thinking is kind of like talking to yourself – just in a way that no one else can hear. And when it comes to motivation, some ways of talking to yourself are probably more helpful than others. Taking a page from the playbook of Steven Safren and colleagues (2017), we want you to think about *how you coach yourself* and whether it's possible to practice and learn more helpful ways of self-coaching.

Let's do a thinking exercise: First, think about the teacher, coach, or mentor in your life **who has motivated and taught you the most**. Reflect on how they did what they did. Why were they so effective at helping you learn and grow?

Teacher/Coach/Mentor Name: _____

What did they teach you? _____

What did they say and do that made them effective?_____

_____

_____

_____

Now, let's think about the flip side: What about a teacher, coach, or mentor who was **least effective** in motivating or teaching you?

Teacher/Coach/Mentor Name: _____

What were they trying to teach you? _____

What did they say or do that made them ineffective? _____

_____

_____

_____

When we thought about *our own* best teachers and coaches, three characteristics came to mind: Good coaches are **encouraging**, **realistic**, and they **teach good strategies**.

Encouraging: An effective coach doesn't berate you to the point of making you feel like there's no point in trying. Instead, they inspire you with the possibility that you can do better. They understand that progress takes time.

Realistic: On the other hand, an effective coach doesn't ignore the reality of what's <u>not</u> working. They don't ignore the problems you're having just to make you feel better. They understand that making you aware of what's going wrong is an important part of helping you improve.

Give Good Strategies: An effective coach doesn't just identify what's not working and give you vague encouragement to "do better". They suggest alternative techniques and help you practice those techniques until you can do them well.

Do you see any evidence of these three qualities in your "best coach" description? Or do you see their opposites in the "worst coach" description?

For example, one coach might point out and highlight every mistake you make, fail to suggest ways to improve, or even bully and berate you under the guise of "motivating". We'll call this guy

Coach Jerkface. Another coach might shower you with praise no matter what and expect very little from you, failing to provide constructive feedback that could lead to progress. This person could be called **Coach Cool Guy**. Very different styles, to be sure, but in the end neither is probably going to be very effective at helping most people learn and grow.

What about the way you coached yourself this past week? Take a look back at your *Noticing Your Patterns* sheet and what you wrote. Check out the following chart for examples of the telltale signs of each of the two coaches we just talked about. See any evidence of pulling a Coach Jerkface on yourself this past week? Or how about Coach Cool Guy? Are there situations where you might have been unrealistically sunny about things in a way that keep you from using skills or dealing with problems?

Examples of Less Helpful Coaching

Coach Jerkface	Coach Cool Guy
That was the worst. Ever.	I have plenty of time to do that later.
Why do I even bother to try?	This usually sucks me in, but I'll just do it for a minute.
That was a complete disaster.	It's not the right time to work on that now.
Everyone thinks I'm incompetent.	Being impulsive is just who I am.
Something bad will happen.	I don't really need to write that down.
I absolutely cannot handle this.	I can remember things on my own.
No one will ever understand me.	I never had to study in high school.
I'm such a loser.	It'll get done.
You're going to screw it up.	I don't need any help.

If thoughts like these seem familiar, guess what? You are HUMAN! Most people experience overly negative (and unhelpful) or overly positive (and also unhelpful) patterns of thinking and feeling from time to time. The key is to do what you're doing now – become aware of these patterns – and then do what comes next: *practice coaching yourself and responding differently.*

Like any new skill, this self-coaching is going to take some practice. Just for fun and maybe to help you remember, we encourage you to give your better coaching style a name – maybe even pay tribute to that best coach or teacher who had such an impact on you.

I'll name my "Good Coach", Coach _____.

Next, check out some examples of more helpful coaching statements provided here. Notice how they are:

• Encouraging
• Realistic
• Suggesting good strategies

Better Coaching Examples

That was *not* great but I can do better. I'm going to try _____ next time.
I did my best with what I had that time, but next time I'll _____.
I've handled tough things before. Maybe it's time to reach out to _____ for help.
I know I'm not the only one who struggles with this stuff. Maybe _____ has some tips for me.
I'm definitely a work in progress.
I may not get it on the first shot, but I'll give it my best try.
I should probably just get the first couple of steps of this done now while I still have some momentum.
I know I have trouble stopping this activity, so I'm going to set a timer for five minutes.
I know I *think* I'm going to remember this, but that's what I always think. I should probably put it in my planner.
I know _____ is really good at this, so I think I'll ask them for help. It feels like I'm bugging them, but I know I like it when someone asks for my expertise.
This assignment has a LOT of parts so I probably need to make a plan to tackle it.

Creating New Responses

Now it's your turn to try creating some helpful self-coaching responses. **Look back at your Noticing Your Patterns** sheet from the last module and choose situation-thought-emotion-action examples from the past week. Copy what you wrote for the first five columns in the following Practicing New Responses table (using shorthand is okay), and then formulate an alternative, more effective self-coaching statement and action and add it to the last column. We've given you an example to help you get started.

Practicing New Responses

Situation – when and where?	Feelings	Thoughts	Action	Why was this action problematic?	Alternative coaching and actions
EXAMPLE: In my dorm room; 10 p.m. on Sunday. Paper due tomorrow at 5 p.m. and I've been putting it off for hours.	guilty UGH! overwhelmed	I don't want to do this! I should have started hours ago. This is going to suck. I need to have this desk clean before I can get started.	Spent 45 min. organizing my desk	I needed to be working on my paper. Organizing the desk ended up making me feel worse in the long run.	I wasted some time, but that's not the end of the world. I'm going to set a timer and work on this section of the paper for 30 minutes, then let myself tidy the desk for 10 min.

As you become more aware, you may notice specific Coach Jerkface or Coach Cool Guy thoughts coming up over and over. We sometimes call these "Red Flag Thoughts" and they can be pretty useful in practicing new responses.

How? Basically, if you can identify a familiar Red Flag Thought when it arises, you can use that as a signal that your alternative responses are probably necessary. For example, if you find yourself frequently thinking, "I'll feel like doing that later", but "later" never seems to come, you can use that Red Flag Thought to signal that it's time to engage a strategy, such as working on the task for ten minutes, breaking it down, or scheduling a time for it in your planner.

Can you identify any Red Flag Thoughts yet? If so, jot them down below for future reference:

_____

_____

_____

Practicing New Responses

Using the sheet on the next page, at least once per day for a few days, fill in the situation and thoughts, feelings, and actions in response, followed by some alternative coaching and actions. It's okay to write down what you *wish* you would have said or done in response to Coach Jerkface or Coach Cool guy, but give yourself some huge extra credit if you can actually think of and carry out those new responses, in the moment. This will get easier the more you make this routine part of your life.

Ask yourself: When would be the best time each day to reflect and, if a situation has happened that day, to fill in your sheet? Then, put it in your calendar!

☐ Check here when you've put this practice on your task list or in your calendar and set a reminder.

Happy Practicing!

Practicing New Responses

Situation – when and where?	Feelings	Thoughts	Action	Why was this action problematic?	Alternative coaching and actions
9:00 at night in my apartment. Saw the dishes piled up in the sink. Had promised my partner I'd take care of them this week.	Exhausted, overwhelmed. A little annoyed.	I am too tired to do this. I've been working ALL DAY. I'm just going to watch TV for a few minutes and then get started.	Watched Nexflix until I fell asleep on the couch.	I watched for longer than I wanted to and didn't get to the dishes. I woke up on the couch feeling terrible, like I let my partner down. Again.	Getting started is ALWAYS the worst part but it'll feel great to have them DONE. I could have propped my phone up on the window sill and watched Netflix while I did the dishes. Or put on a podcast.

Situation – when and where?	Feelings	Thoughts	Action	Why was this action problematic?	Alternative coaching and actions

Module 3.4   Practice New Responses II: Impulsive Emotions

In this module, we'll build on the skills you've developed to address one of the toughest situations out there – **when strong emotions lead to impulsivity: acting without thinking**.

Impulsive Emotions

Your emotions serve many purposes (there are entire college courses on this!) and one of them is to provide motivation to act. This can be a very good thing. Fear can motivate you to escape dangerous situations, anger can motivate you to stand against injustice, and joy can help you lose yourself in a moment of celebration and connection with others. However, moments of strong emotion can also lead to acting in ways that aren't in your best interest, and particularly when you act without thinking through the consequences. This is something psychologists call **impulsivity** and, when impulsivity happens in the presence of strong emotions, it gets to have an even more special set of names. **Negative urgency** refers to the tendency to act without thinking when you're feeling bad and **positive urgency** is the tendency to act without thinking when you're feeling good.

What's the point of knowing all this? The idea here is that, if you can anticipate the kinds of situations where you're likely to feel strong positive or negative emotions, then you can use skills and strategies to help you better manage emotions and allow for the kinds of alternative responses we've been working on so far. And, because emotions can be such a strong influence on our actions, we'll introduce a new tool for helping you do just that.

What kinds of strong emotions have contributed to impulsive actions for you in the past? Complete the following table. We've provided some examples to get you started.

Examples of Strong Emotions and Impulsive Actions

Strong Emotion	*Impulsive Action*	*When Does This Happen?*
Anger	Say mean things I later regret	When I feel like someone is being rude or snarky to me
Excitement	Drinking too much	When partying, especially after a really hard week
Anxiety	Going out with friends when I need to do work	When I have a big assignment due soon and someone asks me to go out
Your Examples:		

So, What Can I Do About This?

Why are we focusing so much on emotions in this module? Can't we just use the kinds of alternative responses we've been practicing earlier in this skillset? Well, if you can, that's fantastic! Do it! But, in our experience, people with ADHD often have times when strong emotions are present and impulsive actions happen so often that they need some extra practice techniques. In other words, these are some of the hardest situations to use alternative responses. . . . But it can be done with specialized methods of practicing.

For these situations, we're going to use a special type of practice that psychologists call *covert rehearsal* or, more commonly, **visualization**. Visualization is often used by sports psychologists to coach athletes on their performance during high-pressure situations. Essentially, you're going to practice your new responses to a situation while you visualize (imagine) it in as much detail as possible, and you're going to do that repeatedly.

Preparing to Visualize

Fill out the following form to set yourself up to visualize. You can find **an additional blank sheet** and **an example of this form**, completed, **at the end of this module**.

I want to practice an alternative response to (*impulsive action that causes problems*):

_____

_____

This action occurs when I'm feeling (*strong emotion*): _____

Now, think about a specific, real-life situation where this impulsive action occurred and you felt the strong emotion. Choose a situation that happened recently or one that you can remember very well. What happened?

_____

_____

Where were you and who was there? What time of day was it?

_____

_____

What did you see, hear, and experience with the five senses? Describe in as much detail as possible:

_____

_____

_____

_____

Describe what the strong emotion you experienced *actually feels like* in your body. If you're not sure, close your eyes for a moment and try to remember what it feels like:

_____

_____

_____

Describe the kinds of thoughts you have when you're feeling this emotion and when the impulsive action occurs:

_____

_____

_____

Now, write down a detailed description of what happened, step by step, and what you experienced including everything mentioned earlier – basically, you want to create a script of the event and what you felt, thought, and did. Make sure you include the impulsive action in your script. If you prefer, you can use your cell phone or computer to record the script instead of writing it out. This is your:

Old Script

_____

_____

_____

_____

_____

Finally, write an alternative version of your script – one where you use alternative coaching, actions, and strategies. For example, what will you say to yourself next time that's realistic, encouraging, and suggests good strategies? What actions can you take to soothe strong emotions? Make sure that in your script you **still include the situation and the strong emotion; just change the way you respond to the strong emotion**. Again, you can write this out or record it. This is your:

New Ending

_____

_____

_____

_____

_____

Practice Time

Now comes the "fun" part. You'll use your script to practice your new response in your head through visualization. Follow these steps:

1) Read or listen to your scripts a few times to get familiar with them.
2) Find a comfortable, quiet place to practice.
3) Relax your body. You can sit or lie down comfortably and you can choose eyes closed or eyes open – do whatever helps you focus inward best. You can use deep breaths or a mindfulness technique from earlier in this skillset to help you relax.
4) Visualize your **Old Script**, step by step, as vividly as possible including all the details from the five senses. Try to really feel the way you felt in the situation and think what you thought.

5) Now, start over and visualize your **Old Script** but with your **New Ending**. Still feel the feelings and think the thoughts, but visualize practicing the alternative thoughts, actions, and strategies you wrote about.

6) **Repeat** your Old Script with New Ending several times. The more you practice, the better!

Ask yourself: When would be the best time this week to practice your visualization? A few days for about 10 minutes at a time should work well. When you've chosen a time, note it in your calendar!

☐ Check here when you've put this practice on your task list or in your calendar and set a reminder.

Slow Your Roll

One last idea for reducing impulsive actions: Sometimes, creating your script and practicing visualization can reveal new ways that you can put some space between your thoughts and emotions and your actions. You basically want to make it *a little bit harder* to take the impulsive action. For example, if you buy things online impulsively, turn off autocomplete for your credit card number. If you snack too much on foods with little nutritional value, don't buy them to stock your dorm fridge. If you respond impulsively with angry emails, set up a dummy email account (laura_is_mad@email.com[2]) to send those emails to first and wait before sending them on (or not). We call these strategies **speed bumps** and they can help derail your usual train of impulsive responding.

Jot down any speed bumps you could set up for your situation:

_____

_____

_____

_____

☐ Check here when you set up these Speed Bumps or put them on your task list or in your calendar and set a reminder.

Happy Visualizing!

Notes

1 Items 1–5 Copyright © 2003 by the American Psychological Association. Reproduced with permission. Brown, K. W., & Ryan, R. M. (2003). The benefits of being present: Mindfulness and its role in psychological well-being. *Journal of Personality and Social Psychology, 84,* 822–848. Items 6–9 Copyright © 2014 by Elsevier. Reproduced with permission. Cyders, M. A., Littlefield, A. K., Coffey, S., & Karyadi, K. A. (2014). Examination of a short English version of the UPPS-P Impulsive Behavior Scale. *Addictive Behaviors, 39*(9), 1372–1376.

2 Not a real email address.

3 This example may or may not be derived from the first author's real-life experience.

References

Brown, K. W., & Ryan, R. M. (2003). The benefits of being present: Mindfulness and its role in psychological well-being. *Journal of Personality and Social Psychology, 84*(4), 822–848. https://doi.org/10.1037/0022-3514.84.4.822

Cyders, M. A., Littlefield, A. K., Coffey, S., & Karyadi, K. A. (2014). Examination of a short English version of the UPPS-P Impulsive Behavior Scale. *Addictive Behaviors, 39*(9), 1372–1376. https://doi.org/10.1016/j.addbeh.2014.02.013

Klein, R., Dubois, S., Gibbons, C., Ozen, L. J., Marshall, S., Cullen, N., & Bédard, M. (2015). The Toronto and Philadelphia mindfulness scales: Associations with satisfaction with life and health-related symptoms. *International Journal of Psychology & Psychological Therapy, 15*(1), 133–142.

Lau, M. A., Bishop, S. R., Segal, Z. V., Buis, T., Anderson, N. D., Carlson, L., Shapiro, S., & Carmody, J. (2006). The Toronto mindfulness scale: Development and validation. *Journal of Clinical Psychology, 62*(12), 1445–1467. https://doi.org/10.1002/jclp.20326

Safren, S. A., Sprich, S., Perlman, C. A., & Otto, M. W. (2017). *Mastering your adult ADHD: A cognitive behavioral treatment program, therapist guide* (2nd ed.). Oxford University Press.

Example:[3] Old Script and New Ending Sheet

I want to practice an alternative response to (impulsive action that causes problems):

Buying things that I don't need (and don't have the money for) on Amazon.

This action occurs when I'm feeling (strong emotion): A little excited, anticipation. And also like things are hard and I deserve something nice.

Describe what this *actually feels like* in your body. If you're not sure, close your eyes for a moment and remember a time you felt that emotion:

I think my heart might beat a little faster and my chest feels a little bit of pressure. Probably my eyes hurt from looking at my phone too long. :(

Describe the kinds of thoughts you have when you're feeling this emotion and when the impulsive action occurs:

This is awesome! I can probably use this for (whatever purpose) and all these people I know will think this is really cool. (Visualize myself using the thing I'm buying, imagine being in that situation.) I really haven't treated myself in a while and I deserve this. I've looked at it three times before and didn't buy it so I must really genuinely want it.

Now, describe a specific, real-life situation where this impulsive action occurred and you felt the strong emotion. Choose a situation that happened recently or one that you can remember very well. What happened?

Lying in my bed at night and scrolling through Instagram and an ad pops up for magnetic eyelashes and I click on it. I've looked at these same ones two or three times before but didn't buy them. Feel like I deserve these. Look through all the different options and put them in my cart and buy five different pairs b/c I just HAVE to have all the types and I'm thinking it is a "deal" to buy the bundle. Then totally forgot I even bought them until they came in the mail. Feel guilty because my credit card bill is already SOOOO high I'm making the minimum payments and I spent $200 on fake lashes. :(

Where were you and who was there? What time of day was it?

Alone in my bed in my dorm after staying up until 2 AM to finish my work.

What did you see, hear, and experience with the five senses? Describe in as much detail as possible:

Dark except for the light coming off of my phone. My eyes hurt from staring at the screen. The stupid air conditioning is making a loud clanking sound as usual and it's too cold so I have all of my covers on. Can't get comfortable in bed. Smells vaguely like burnt popcorn because that happens every other night in this dorm.

Now, write down a detailed description of what happened and what you experienced including everything mentioned earlier – basically, you want to create a script of the event and what you felt, thought, and did. Make sure you include the impulsive action in your script. If you prefer, you can use your cell phone or computer to record the script instead of writing it out. This is your:

Old Script

It's 2 AM on Wednesday. I just finished a response paper for my seminar I'd been putting off for hours. I climb into bed and pull up all my covers like usual because the air conditioning is on full blast, as usual. I can hear it clanking and I try to tune it out. The air still smells like the microwave popcorn somebody on my hall burnt earlier. Everything is dark except for the light coming from my phone and a little bit coming from under the door. I pull up Instagram and start scrolling. And scrolling. My eyes are heavy and they start to sting but my thumb keeps moving anyway. I shift back and forth in my bed as my arm gets too tired to hold the phone.

An ad for MagneLash scrolls up in the feed and I almost miss it, but pull back to click on it. I've looked at these, like, three times before and I've always wanted to try them. I click through page after page of different styles and different kinds of bundles they offer. I feel a little more awake and my chest feels a little tighter with an excited kind of feeling as I explore the options. These look SO COOL and I could wear them out but also some look like they could work for "every day." There are so many options. Keep adding styles to my cart so I don't forget them. I feel totally absorbed in looking at all the options, comparing prices and styles, making sure I find the ones I like the best. Finally, I think I've seen everything and I click back to my cart to narrow down which ones I really want. Dammit, there's, like, six pairs in here and the total is too much. But wait, I saw a promo code . . . buy 4 get the 5th free. Okay, that's a deal. Plus, I have been working hard lately and haven't treated myself in a while. Plus, this is the third time I've looked at these so I must really want them. I'm going for it! I hit the button to check out. When I start entering my credit card number, Google fills the rest in for me, just gotta put in that three digit code. Alright, I gotta actually go to sleep now. I finally plug in my phone, set my alarm, and turn over to go to sleep.

Finally, write an alternative version of your script – one where you use alternative coaching, actions, and strategies. Make sure that in your script you **still include the situation and the strong emotion; just change the way you respond to the strong emotion**. Again, you can write this out or record it. This is your:

New Ending

(Everything the same and then starting at this line): Finally, I think I've seen everything and I click back to my cart to narrow down which ones I really want. Dammit, there's, like, six pairs in here and the total is too much. But wait, I saw a promo code . . . buy 4 get the 5th free. Okay, that's a deal. Plus, I have been working hard lately and haven't treated myself in a while. Plus, this is the third time I've looked at these so I must really want them.

On the other hand, I'm not sure this is the right choice at this moment. I know I have an issue with buying stuff late at night but, at the same time, I might really want these. I'm going to leave this stuff in my cart and then wait until later to decide which ones to buy. So I don't forget, I'll just make a note on my calendar to remind me to come back to the cart. Alright, I gotta actually go to sleep now. I finally plug in my phone, set my alarm, and turn over to go to sleep.

Jot down any speed bumps you could set up for your situation:

Turn off autocomplete for my credit card number. Give myself a budget of Instagram hours per day using an app that my friend told me about so I'm not seeing those ads.

Old Script and New Ending – Visualization Exercise

I want to practice an alternative response to (impulsive action that causes problems):

This action occurs when I'm feeling (strong emotion):

Describe what this *actually feels like* in your body. If you're not sure, close your eyes for a moment and remember a time you felt that emotion:

Describe the kinds of thoughts you have when you're feeling this emotion and when the impulsive action occurs:

Now, describe a specific, real-life situation where this impulsive action occurred and you felt the strong emotion. Choose a situation that happened recently or one that you can remember very well. What happened?

Where were you and who was there? What time of day was it?

What did you see, hear, and experience with the five senses? Describe in as much detail as possible:

Now, write down a detailed description of what happened and what you experienced including everything mentioned earlier – basically, you want to create a script of the event and what you felt, thought, and did. Make sure you include the impulsive action in your script. If you prefer, you can use your cell phone or computer to record the script instead of writing it out. This is your:

Old Script

Finally, write an alternative version of your script – one where you use alternative coaching, actions, and strategies. Make sure that in your script you **still include the situation and the strong emotion; just change the way you respond to the strong emotion**. Again, you can write this out or record it. This is your:

New Ending

Jot down any speed bumps you could set up for your situation:

Finally, go back to page **85** and follow the instructions for visualization practice in the section labeled "Practice Time".

4 Taking Good Care of Yourself

Module 4.0 Why It Matters and Roadmap

In college, taking good care of your health and well-being (e.g., eating well, sleeping well, exercising regularly) is an area you need to manage on your own now more than ever. College is a time when students are learning to be even more independent from their parents than they were in high school and this means that they have to do more for themselves. Lots of college students struggle with this extra responsibility (regardless of whether they have ADHD or not). Students with ADHD might struggle even more because these areas of life require organization and planning. For example, eating healthy requires meal planning, grocery shopping, and cooking whereas ordering DoorDash is quick and easy; however, ordering take out and purchasing fast food is also more expensive and usually less healthy. When you get busy, it's easy to let these areas of life slide and not make them a priority. But research also shows that doing your best work in college relies on keeping your body and mind healthy. In this section, we are going to discuss six areas of self-care (i.e., sleep, eating, exercise, substances, technology, and driving). You will decide if you want to make changes in any of these areas, and if now is the right time for you, we will provide you with some ideas for making changes.

Check Yourself: What's Your Target?

Think about each of the six major health and lifestyle areas listed here, and write a few sentences about how you are doing right now in each of these areas. What is going well, and what's causing problems for you in your life right now?

Thoughts about my sleep habits:

Thoughts about my eating habits and nutrition:

Thoughts about my exercise and level of physical activity:

DOI: 10.4324/9781003149620-5

Thoughts about my use of alcohol, nicotine, and other drugs:

Thoughts about my technology use (e.g., phone, internet, video games):

Thoughts about my driving (e.g., speeding, texting, driving under the influence):

Now, based on what you wrote, answer the following questions:

Which lifestyle area is currently **causing the most problems** in your life (check one)?

❏ Sleep ❏ Eating and Nutrition ❏ Exercise and Physical Activities ❏ Alcohol and Drug Use
❏ Technology Use ❏ Driving Safely

Which lifestyle area are you currently **managing the most effectively** (check one)?

❏ Sleep ❏ Eating and Nutrition ❏ Exercise and Physical Activities ❏ Alcohol and Drug Use
❏ Technology Use ❏ Driving Safely

Which lifestyle area do you feel **most capable of changing right now** (check one)?

❏ Sleep ❏ Eating and Nutrition ❏ Exercise and Physical Activities ❏ Alcohol and Drug Use
❏ Technology Use ❏ Driving Safely

Looking back on your answers, which area **would you like to commit to working on right now**?

 Remember, it is okay to commit to *small changes* to start!

I'll commit to working on: _____

Make Your Plan

1. **Put a "1" next to the module that you just wrote down** (the one you're committing to).
2. **Include any additional modules that you think might be helpful** or that you're curious about, **adding numbers 2 through 6 to indicate your priorities.** (You <u>don't</u> need to include <u>all</u> the modules in your plan.)
3. **Work on the modules you selected in priority order** by adding each module to your **task list and/or calendar** and tackling them one at a time. Check off each module when you finish it and **reward yourself for a job well done**!

Health and Well-Being Skills Plan

In my plan? 1 = first priority	Done	Module	Pages
		Module 4.1. *Sleeping Better*	**95–99**
		Module 4.2. *Eating Healthier*	**100–104**
		Module 4.3. *Increasing Physical Activity*	**104–106**
		Module 4.4. *Managing Substance Use*	**106–109**
		Module 4.5. *Managing Technology Use*	**110–112**
		Module 4.6 *Driving Safely*	**112–115**

 A lot of the skills and strategies in this module will build on the organization and time management skills introduced in Skill 1 of this workbook. Therefore, if you haven't already gone through the modules in Skill 1, we encourage you to spend some time with those before you tackle these.

Module 4.1   Sleeping Better

Congratulations! You've made the commitment to working on one of the most important lifestyle areas for physical and emotional health: your sleep. Up to half of people with ADHD experience sleep problems (Wajszilber et al., 2018) and it's no secret that sleep deprivation can make you feel terrible and make problems with concentration and motivation worse. As the semester goes on, students sometimes end up staying awake later and later to finish their work, which shifts their sleep cycle and interferes with activities during the day. Napping during the day can actually end up making this pattern worse.

This module contains three sets of skills that might help you sleep longer and better. For each skill, first answer the questions and then review the strategies that might be helpful.

Setting the Stage for Sleep

Describe what you generally do in the 30 minutes before getting into bed:

_____

_____

Do you use your phone, tablet, or laptop in bed before going to sleep?

- ☐ Always or almost always
- ☐ Sometimes
- ☐ Never

Do you watch TV or use the internet in bed before going to sleep?

- ☐ Always or almost always
- ☐ Sometimes
- ☐ Never

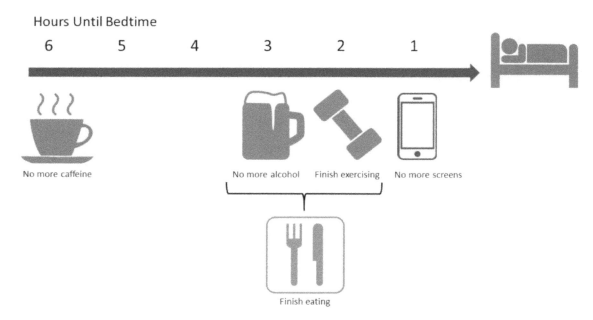

Figure 4.1 Preparing for good sleep.

Now, look back at your answers. Are you doing a good job of signaling your body that it's time to power down? Check out Figure 4.1 for some ideas about how best to prepare your body and mind for sleep.

We've found that **using screens in bed** has a particularly negative effect on sleep. So, if you're habitually using screens in bed, there's a strong possibility that this is contributing to your sleep difficulties – especially if you're using screens for a long time before falling asleep. If this sounds like you, check the box here and definitely add this strategy to your list:

☐ ***Keep phone/tablet/laptop and charger out of reach while in bed (e.g., across the room). You can use wireless headphones if you want to listen to something**.

Next, review the list of other stage-setting strategies here and check any that interest you.

☐ ***Read a book or listen to low-key music or spoken word before falling asleep**
☐ ***Use earplugs or white noise to block out distracting sound**
☐ ***Make your room very dark by using blackout shades and keeping lamps off when possible**
☐ ***Skip the caffeine, alcohol, and nicotine close to bedtime**
☐ ***Make sure your pillow is comfortable and supportive**

Responding to Sleeplessness

When I get into bed at night, it typically takes me _____ to fall asleep.

☐ 15 minutes or less
☐ 15–60 minutes
☐ More than 60 minutes

Is waking up in the middle of the night and not being able to fall back asleep ever a problem?

☐   No
☐   Yes – If yes, how often does this occur and what do you do when you wake up at night?
_____

Occasional bouts of sleeplessness can become a pattern if your body starts to connect being alert to being in bed. When you feel like you can't fall asleep, it's tempting to just lie there waiting for things to change. Instead, consider the following strategy and check it off if it seems relevant to you, based on your previous answers.

☐   ***If you're lying in bed and haven't fallen asleep after <u>about</u> 20 minutes, get out of bed and do something relaxing (no screens!) until you begin to feel sleepy. Then try again**.
When you try again, avoid watching the time. Tell yourself, "As long as I'm resting, I will be fine".

Fixing a Faulty Cycle

During the week, I generally go to bed at _____ and wake up at _____,
    which results in about _____ hours of sleep per night.
On the weekends, I generally go to bed at _____ and wake up at _____,
    which results in about _____ hours of sleep per night.

My current sleep/wake times are:

☐   A great fit with my schedule of activities
☐   An okay fit with my schedule of activities
☐   A terrible fit with my schedule and I'd like to change them

The times I go to bed and wake up are:

☐   Always consistent, I stick to a schedule
☐   Fairly consistent from day to day with some variations
☐   All over the place

How often do you experience daytime sleepiness?

☐   Never or almost never
☐   Sometimes
☐   Daily or almost daily

How often do you nap during the day?

☐   Never or almost never
☐   Sometimes, almost daily, or daily

    How long are your naps? _____

When you nap, are you trying to "make up" for not sleeping enough at night?

☐ Yes
☐ No

Look back at your answers. Does your sleep cycle need a reset? When you get in the pattern of going to sleep later and later at night, your body wants to stay asleep later in the morning, which interferes with your daytime activities. If you chronically don't get enough sleep, you end up feeling sleepy during the day and then, possibly, taking lengthy daytime naps that push your natural "sleepy time" back even further into the night.

To make progress in re-setting your sleep cycle, you'll need to take the following steps:

☐ ***Choose a target bedtime – something closer to your ideal but still realistic** (Keep in mind that most young adults' natural sleep cycle involves falling asleep pretty late at night, so it might not be reasonable to select a 10 p.m. bedtime if your usual fall-asleep time is 2 a.m., but picking a 12:30 a.m. bedtime might be more reasonable): _____
☐ ***Choose a target wake-up time:** _____
☐ ***Put these bedtimes and wake times into your calendar** *at the same times each day* **even if you don't think you can always stick to them yet**
☐ ***If you think napping is messing with your sleep cycle, avoid it as much as possible.** If you feel super sleepy at any point during the day, it can help to get up and move around. Take a walk or even just do some jumping jacks in place.

Each Night, Follow a Reset Plan

*Sleep Reset Plan

1) Get in bed 30 minutes earlier than the typical time you fall asleep, using good stage-setting strategies (and no phone!)
2) If you don't fall asleep after about 20 minutes, get up and do something relaxing and screen free until you begin to feel sleepy. This might take a while sometimes.
3) Get back in bed and try again. No need to obsessively watch the time. Use positive statements to soothe anxiety, "As long as I am resting, it will be okay".
4) Repeat steps 2) and 3) as needed.
5) Wake up at your target wake time and get out of bed immediately. (Maybe to retrieve your phone?)
6) The following night, get in bed 30 minutes earlier than when you fell asleep the prior night, gradually moving toward your target bed time.

After a while, your sleep cycle will hopefully begin to move back in line with the ideal.

📖 We've based our tips in this module on cognitive-behavioral therapy for insomnia (CBT-I). If you have trouble following this plan or if you need additional support, digital CBT-I can be helpful (Tsai et al., 2022). Try searching for "CBT insomnia app" or "CBT insomnia online" to find programs. You might also find additional support through your college's counseling center.

Pulling Together Your Sleep Plan

On the next page, we've pulled together all of the sleep strategies from this skillset into one handy chart that you can use to make your own personal sleep plan. Review the strategy items you checked off earlier, in **boldface** and marked with a *, and check off these items on the sleep plan sheet. Then, put the first items on your calendar or task list.
   Happy Sleeping!

Personal Sleep Plan

Based on your answers on the previous pages, check off the sleep strategies that you'll make part of your sleep plan. In the skillset, these are **in boldface and marked with a ***. Then, put these as items in your calendar or task list, setting a reminder if appropriate, and tackle the first strategy **right now**!

In Your Plan? (X)	*Strategy*	*Page Number*	*In Calendar/ Task List?*
	Move phone/tablet/laptop and charger out of reach while in bed (e.g., across the room).	p. 96	
	Read a book or listen to low-key music or spoken word before falling asleep (NO SCREENS)	p. 96	
	Use earplugs or white noise to block out distracting sound	p. 96	
	Make your room very dark by using blackout shades and keeping lamps off when possible	p. 96	
	Skip the caffeine, alcohol, and nicotine close to bedtime	p. 96	
	Make sure your pillow is comfortable and supportive	p. 96	
	If you can't fall asleep after 20 minutes, get out of bed and do something relaxing (no screens!) until you begin to feel sleepy. Then try again but avoid obsessively watching the clock and be sure to use positive self-talk ("As long as I am resting, it will be fine").	p. 97	
	Choose a consistent bedtime and wake-up time and put them in your calendar	p. 98	
	Avoid daytime naps	p. 98	
	Try the **Sleep Reset Plan**	p. 98	
	Download and use an app based on cognitive-behavioral therapy for insomnia (I-CBT)		
	Get an appointment for CBT-I at your college counseling center (if they don't offer this treatment, you could ask them to refer you to a community therapist)		

Module 4.2 Eating Healthier

There's been a long-standing debate about the role of diet in ADHD. To make a long story short, we know that diet doesn't cause ADHD – for example, that sugar doesn't actually make kids more hyperactive – but there is some decent evidence that your eating habits can have an impact on the way you feel and how well you can pay attention. Because good nutrition is important for your health in general, there's little risk (and lots of potential reward) in targeting your eating habits for improvement.

What to Eat?

There's no evidence that diet or sugar causes ADHD (Hoover & Milich, 1994) or that extremely specialized diets are helpful for ADHD. However, general guidelines for a diet rich in vitamins, minerals, and fiber – including fresh vegetables and ample protein sources – and fewer processed foods are probably a solid bet, regardless of your ADHD. Avoiding added sugar (as in soda and other sugar-sweetened beverages), saturated fats (in many packaged snack foods), and excessive caffeine is probably also a good choice. When it comes to taking vitamins and other supplements, there's not clear evidence for effects of specific nutrients in impacting ADHD symptoms; however, there's some evidence of a small effect of omega-3 fatty acid supplements on improving behavior in children with ADHD (Nigg, 2018). So, if these aren't too expensive for you and you're not using them to replace other ADHD treatments, they might be worth a shot. Above all, **you should consult with your doctor or a nutritionist when making decisions about your diet.** Many colleges have dieticians or nutritionists on staff, who can do individual consultations with students – something to check out!

Next, rather than focusing on what you shouldn't eat, begin thinking about what you'd like to eat more of by responding to the questions here.

What foods do you currently **eat too little of or not often enough** – good-for-you foods you want to increase your intake of? Only write down *foods you actually don't mind eating* but don't consume often right now.[1] Consider including at least one fruit and one veggie on this list.

- _____
- _____
- _____
- _____
- _____
- _____
- _____

What foods (or sugar-sweetened drinks, like sodas) do you currently **eat or drink too often or too much of** that you'd like to cut back on? In other words, what are your "worst offenders?"

- _____
- _____

- _____
- _____
- _____
- _____
- _____

Good job – we'll come back to these shortly.

A Word of Caution . . .

 The strategies we cover in this section are designed to help people make healthier nutritional choices; however, they are not designed to help people who are experiencing eating disorders that involve excessive restriction of food, struggles with body image, excessive food intake that is hard to control (bingeing) or problematic efforts to lose weight (e.g., purging). If you suspect that you may be experiencing an eating disorder, please call the National Eating Disorders Association Helpline at (800) 931–2237 and make an appointment at your University's counseling center as soon as possible. Help is available!

How to Eat?

In some ways, figuring out what to eat is the easy part. If that were the only step, everyone's diet would be a lot healthier. The problem is that *our food environments are set up to sabotage us*. Think about it – less nutritious food is often cheaper, more convenient, more heavily advertised, and full of the sugar, salt, and fat that makes it taste extra yummy. So when you're tired, stressed out, or off of your routine, it's easy to reach for something convenient that's also LESS likely to be nutritious.

So, to eat better, you'll need to lower some of the barriers to making healthier choices, put up some barriers around the less healthy choices, and figure out strategies to address those situations where you're vulnerable to getting off track. As much as possible, the goal is to *eat with a plan instead of eating on impulse*. This won't be easy but, fortunately, you can apply some of the skills we've covered earlier in the workbook to help.

We've grouped the skills and strategies for healthy eating into three groups:

- Planning Ahead – Strategies to set yourself up to make healthy choices
- Keeping on Track – Strategies to help you stick to your plan
- Addressing Triggers – Strategies to discover and address thoughts and feelings that lead to less healthy choices

In the next sections, read up on each menu of strategies (see what we did there?!) and decide which ones you want to add to your personal eating plan.

Plan Ahead Strategies

> Craig is so busy all the time that he rarely even remembers to stop to eat. Sometimes, by the end of the day, he ends up so hungry that he orders DoorDash on the way home from his late evening class. Other times, he visits the campus convenience store for chips and a soda to eat on the go. When he does stock up on a few items for his off campus apartment, he picks microwave meals and instant ramen noodles for a quick meal. And pizza delivery is always a couple of app clicks away.

Craig's main challenge seems to be carving out a regular schedule for eating and planning ahead so that he's not leaving himself with no alternative but to eat less nutritious convenience food and sodas. If Craig's challenges sound like yours, review the following strategies and check off those you'd like to try. You don't have to try everything – just choose the strategies that you think might fit into your lifestyle.

☐ Block off times for meals in your calendar and add reminders to prevent skipping. However, keep in mind that you should only eat when you are actually hungry.

☐ Add the foods you identified earlier in the chapter – your "worst offenders" – to a Don't Buy List and post the list on your phone or in your kitchen. Consider including sugar-sweetened beverages (e.g., soda) on your Don't Buy List.

☐ Stock up on a few of the tastier foods you listed at the start of this chapter that you're not eating as much of. When you're hungry, they'll be there for you.

☐ Choose a day of the week to plan your meals and grocery shop and put it in your calendar

☐ Prep snacks and meal elements for grab-and-go convenience. For example, cut up fruits, veggies, or cheese in advance to snack on easily. Keep a few healthy snacks in your backpack.

☐ When you have time to cook, prepare extra meal portions and freeze them for a quick, healthy meal later.

Keep on Track Strategies

> Anita always starts a new semester with the best of intentions to eat better. For the first week or so, she only consumes "healthy" foods from the vegetarian section of the dining hall. Before too long, though, Anita is persuaded by her friends to eat out more and more often, where it's harder to make healthy choices. Once Anita feels like she's fallen off the healthy eating train, she stops paying attention to her diet altogether until the start of the next semester.

Anita's main issue seems to be maintaining healthy patterns as things get more hectic. If Anita's struggles sound familiar, consider the following:

☐ Download a food log app, such as MyFitnessPal or MyPlate, and use it to track what you're eating. Psychologists call this *self-monitoring* and it's one of the most effective ways to maintain healthy eating over time.

☐ Develop a few healthy eating strategies that can be maintained over time, for example eat a fruit or veggie appetizer (but not dried or juice) before meals twice a day.

☐ Set an eating out budget – either a dollar amount or a number of outings per month – and track it. When you run out for the month, no more eating out until the next month rolls around.

☐ Experiment with time-restricted eating. Specifically, set a daily eating window for yourself (e.g., I will eat from 10 a.m. to 10 p.m. each day but not after 10 p.m.). A lot of people find that they eat the most problematic foods late at night.

Addressing Triggers

Diego does pretty well with his eating habits when things are going well, but when he gets stressed out or feels like he's too busy to do other fun things, he tends to eat more desserts and other sugary foods like cookies and ice cream. When feeling particularly stressed out, frustrated, or busy, he notices himself often having the thought: "I deserve to treat myself. I've worked hard today!" and following that up with a trip to the on campus convenience store for a pint of Ben & Jerry's or a quick trip off campus for a shake at Sonic. After eating sweets, Diego feels more relaxed, but later wishes he'd made a different choice.

Diego's main challenge seems to be that his eating is strongly linked to certain thoughts and emotions. If this challenge seems familiar to you, consider the following:

☐ Use the material in Module 3.3 to figure out if any specific thoughts are getting in the way of your healthy eating and develop and practice new responses to those thoughts.

☐ Use the material in Module 3.4 to figure out if your eating is related to impulsive emotions and develop and practice new responses to these impulsive emotions.

☐ Consider subscribing to Noom, a research-based healthy eating Smartphone application.

Make Your Plan

Now that you've reviewed some possible strategies, it's time to make your plan. Look back at the things you checked off and add them to your personal eating plan on the next page. Make sure to put these goals, strategies, and steps into your calendar and onto your task list.

Happy Healthy Eating!

Personal Eating Plan

Based on your answers on the previous pages, check off the healthy eating strategies that you'll make part of your plan. Then, put these as items in your calendar or task list, setting a reminder if appropriate, and tackle the first strategy **right now**!

In Your Plan? (X)	Strategy	In Calendar / Task List?
	Make an appointment with your University's dietician or nutritionist	
	Block off times for meals in your calendar and add reminders	
	Make a food Don't Buy List and instead buy tasty and healthy alternatives to have on hand	
	Choose a day of the week to plan your meals and grocery shop	
	Prep snacks and meal elements for grab-and-go convenience Keep a few healthy snacks in your backpack	
	When you have time to cook, prepare extra meal portions and freeze them for a quick, healthy meal later	
	Download a food log app and track what you eat	
	Set an eating out budget and stick to it	
	Set a daily time window for your eating (e.g., until 10 p.m.) and put a reminder on your phone or calendar	
	Develop a few healthy eating strategies that can be maintained over time, for example eat a fruit or veggie appetizer (but not dried or juice) before meals twice a day	
	Use Skillset 3.4 to identify and address thinking patterns related to less healthy eating choices	
	Use Skillset 3.5 to identify and address impulsive emotions related to less healthy eating choices	
	Consider subscribing to Noom, a research-based healthy eating Smartphone application	

Put an "X" in the column if it's in your plan

Module 4.3   Increasing Physical Activity

There are several ways in which physical activity levels and ADHD symptoms might influence one another. Before describing these, we will define some terms. First, physical activity includes any movement that results in increased energy expenditure. This includes activity while working (e.g., sitting, standing, lifting) and engaging in household and leisure activities (e.g., walking, household tasks, sports, metabolic conditioning exercises). Physical exercise is a subtype of physical activity and includes any activity that is engaged in for the purpose of developing or maintaining physical fitness (e.g., playing sports, weightlifting, running, swimming, cycling). Exercise has been shown to improve physical (e.g., cardiovascular disease, diabetes) and psychological (e.g., anxiety, depression) problems (Hillman et al., 2008). Due to these benefits, the U.S. Department of Health and Human Services (2018) has recommended that adults engage in at least 150 minutes of moderate intensity exercise per week (e.g., 30 minutes × 5 days per week, 50 minutes × 3 days per week, or 75 minutes × 2 days per week). However, only 23.2% of adults in the United States meet these criteria. Thus, many of us should be working toward increasing our exercise.

Research showing an impact on ADHD is fairly new and there is not yet a lot of it. Some studies show that exercise helps improve symptoms of ADHD in young adults immediately following a bout of exercise (LaCount et al., 2022) and some research has also found that exercise helps with anxiety and depression (Rebar et al., 2015). Given that anxiety and depression are often also present in individuals with ADHD, exercise may have multiple benefits for college students with ADHD.

In spite of the potential for positive impact on physical and mental health, it may be especially challenging for college students with ADHD to establish a regular exercise routine. Specifically, problems with organization, time management, and planning may interfere with completing necessary tasks (e.g., school work, housework) and it may be even more difficult to make time for exercise. So, in this module, you'll want to build on your skills from Skillset 1 to help increase your motivation and create time for exercise.

Assess Your Physical Activity

What Are Your Current Physical Activity Routines?

- How many days per week do you exercise?
- How often do you walk or bike for transportation?
- How many times per week do you exercise?
- When you exercise, how long do your workouts usually last?
- What types of activities do you do for exercise?
- How satisfied are you with your current habits?
- Would you like to make a change?
- If so, what kind of change would you like to make (e.g., Would you like to exercise more or less?)
- If yes, why would you like to make a change (e.g., health, academics, relationships)?
- How confident are you about your ability to make a change in this area at this time?

Physical Activity Strategies

Which of the Following Strategies Do You Use, Have You Tried, or Would You Be Willing to Try?

- ☐ Walk or bike to work or on errands if feasible.
- ☐ Take the stairs instead of the elevator.
- ☐ Park further away from the store on purpose.
- ☐ Use an activity or step tracker (e.g., FitBit, Garmin watch, Apple watch) with a smartphone app and set a daily steps goal.
- ☐ Set a goal for how many times per week you would like to exercise. Think about whether you want to focus on further, longer or faster.
- ☐ Put exercise on your calendar and build into your day.
- ☐ Consider whether you prefer working out alone or with others.
- ☐ Find an accountability or work-out partner (e.g., make plans to work out with a friend to increase the likelihood that you will follow through). If your friend is at a different skill level, you could have a plan to go together but not exercise together (e.g., swim at different speeds).

☐ Consider joining a yoga studio or a gym. This can be helpful if you do not have a reliable workout partner because you might develop acquaintances or friendships at the gym and you might look forward to seeing these folks. You might also be more likely to go to an exercise class if you have already paid for it in advance.

☐ Pick physical activities that you enjoy doing or that you find less aversive (e.g., if you dislike running, start with walking).

☐ Listen to music or an audiobook while exercising to make the experience more pleasant and consider <u>only</u> allowing yourself to listen to them while exercising.

☐ Join a club or a class to learn a new activity (e.g., take an introduction to cross-country skiing or canoeing at your campus outdoor program, attend a group workout class at your campus recreation center).

☐ Schedule exercise more frequently to plan for the inevitable times when it doesn't work out due to other more urgent tasks (e.g., if you want to exercise 3 times per week, then schedule 5 times knowing that you can skip 2 if the timing isn't working out).

☐ Use a smartphone app that allows you to see what your friends and acquaintances are doing for exercise (e.g., Strava).

☐ Reward yourself for meeting your daily steps goal or increasing your exercise sessions, perhaps with a new work-out outfit, tennis shoes, or a healthy smoothie.

Go for It!

For the physical activity goals that you have chosen to work on first, identify one to three strategies from the aforementioned list that you will try this week.

☐ Check here when they're added to your calendar and task list.

Module 4.4   Managing Substance Use

College students with ADHD have more problems with drinking than college students without ADHD. Although substance use often results in immediate positive feelings, research shows longer-term negative effects on physical and mental health (e.g., tiredness, lethargy, negative mood), academic performance, and social relationships. Research also shows that some ADHD-like symptoms (e.g., difficulty concentrating, low motivation) can be completely accounted for by heavy substance use. For those with a previous diagnosis, research suggests that substance use might make ADHD symptoms worse. For these reasons, college students with ADHD may wish to monitor and reduce their use of alcohol, nicotine (e.g., vaping), marijuana, or other substances.

Reasons for Substance Use

Drinking motives have been studied based on type of reinforcement (to feel good versus escape from feeling bad) and source of motivation (internal or external). By crossing these two dimensions, researchers have found four drinking motives:

1. **Drinking to cope with stress** involves negative reinforcement (e.g., drinking is rewarding because negative emotions decrease temporarily) and internal motivation (e.g., drinking to feel differently).
2. **Drinking to enhance mood** involves positive reinforcement (e.g., drinking is rewarding because positive emotions increase temporarily) and internal motivation (e.g., drinking to feel differently).
3. **Drinking for social reasons** involves positive reinforcement (e.g., drinking is rewarding because positive emotions increase temporarily) and external motivation (e.g., drinking to increase sociability or other people's impressions).
4. **Drinking to conform** involves negative reinforcement (e.g., drinking is rewarding because negative emotions decrease temporarily) and external motivation (e.g., drinking to manage other people's impressions).

Research shows that drinking to cope or conform socially predicts alcohol-related problems and that drinking to cope and enhance mood predict heavy drinking (Kuntsche et al., 2005). Thus, the *least* unhealthy reason is **drinking for social reasons** (e.g., celebrating). Similar motives may also be applied to the use of other substances (e.g., vaping, nicotine, marijuana) although less work has been done.

Harm Reduction

The harm reduction approach to substance use is in contrast to the abstinence approach. You may be familiar with Drug Abuse Resistance Education (DARE) or Alcoholics Anonymous (AA). DARE and AA are abstinence-based approaches to the prevention and treatment of substance abuse. They are focused on *avoiding or completely eliminating* the use of substances. In contrast, harm reduction is focused on providing education so that individuals can make informed choices and, if they choose, use substances safely and in moderation.

One example of the use of harm reduction is how young people learn to drive in the United States. In order to get your driver's license, you have to take a class, get insurance, practice with your parents, wear your seatbelt, and take a test. We acknowledge that driving can be dangerous and we help adolescents learn how to drive safely to reduce the risks. Another example is the "safe sex" approach to sex education. Although there is still societal debate over whether to use a safe sex or abstinence approach to sex education, the research is very clear that the safe sex, or harm reduction approach, is most effective. We take a similar approach to drinking and substance use.

The goals of harm reduction are to educate individuals regarding the true dangers of substance use rather than fear-based exaggerations. Specifically, the goals are to maximize enjoyment, minimize risk, and minimize after effects. For example, if you drink for social reasons, how much alcohol should you drink over the course of the evening to maximize fun while minimizing the risks (e.g., throwing up, saying or doing things you might regret, or feeling sick or unmotivated the following day)? The National Institute on Alcohol Use and Alcoholism (NIAAA) (Looby et al., 2021) has developed a definition of heavy drinking. Specifically, for men, consuming more than four drinks on any day or more than 14 drinks per week is considered heavy drinking. For women, consuming more than three drinks on any day or more than seven drinks per week is considered heavy drinking. These sex differences are based not only on the larger average size of men than women but also on differences in metabolism. There are immediate and long-term risks associated with heavy drinking. Therefore, it is recommended that those who drink aim to stay in the low to moderate range, which may be especially challenging for college students given the drinking culture on some campuses. In addition, there are several other harm reduction strategies you can use.

Research suggests that there are some very specific behavioral strategies that college students with elevated ADHD symptoms can engage in that may reduce problems associated with alcohol use, such as missing class, being hungover, DUIs, and other undesirable outcomes related to heavy use (Looby et al., 2021). These are called protective behavioral strategies (PBS). Examples of such strategies are setting a predetermined time to stop drinking, having beers or mixed drinks instead of shots, and avoiding drinking games. Next, we will describe these behavioral strategies in more detail as well as other ways to reduce substance use and associated problems.

Assess Your Substance Use

What Are Your Current Substance Use Habits?

How many days per week do you use alcohol?

When you drink, how many drinks do you have?

How many days per week do you use marijuana?

When you use marijuana, how much do you use?

Do you use any other substances?

Does using substances cause any problems for you, like missing class, being hungover, blacking out, getting into arguments or fights, or driving under the influence?

How satisfied are you with your current substance use habits?

Would you like to make a change?

> If so, what change would you like to make?
> If so, why would you like to make a change (e.g., health, academics, relationships)?
> How confident are you about your ability to make a change in this area at this time?

Substance Use Harm Reduction Strategies

Which of the Following Strategies Do You Use, Have You Tried, or Would You Be Willing to Try?

There are a number of protective behavioral strategies that have been shown through research to be helpful to college students with **ADHD** for reducing alcohol use and the negative outcomes associated with use such as blacking out, being hungover, driving drunk, and missing class. Check off the strategies that you think will be most helpful for you.

☐ Track your use of alcohol and drugs. Set a goal of reducing use. Reward yourself for progress in this area, perhaps with a fun activity with friends that does not involve drinking or using drugs like playing paintball, going out for coffee, or taking a walk.

☐ Set a limit on the number of drinks you will have in one drinking session. If you don't think you can keep track, put that many rubber bands on one wrist and each time you have a drink, remove a rubber band and put it in your pocket.

☐ Mix and bring your own beverages. When what you bought is gone, stop drinking.

☐ Avoid combining alcohol and marijuana. Combining substances can make you get more drunk/high and reduce your ability to make good decisions about limiting your use and staying safe.

☐ Avoid pre-gaming or pre-partying.

☐ Stop drinking at a predetermined time and drink water only after this time. This will also help you sleep better.

☐ Eat a meal before or during drinking.

☐ Avoid mixing different types of alcohol.

☐ Drink slowly rather than gulping or chugging. If you feel pressure to drink more, you can always pretend to take a sip now and then. You can also take your drink to the kitchen or bathroom or outside and pour some out.

☐ Avoid trying to keep up or out drink others. Avoid drinking games.

☐ Alternate alcoholic and nonalcoholic drinks. For every alcoholic drink you have, drink a glass of water. Or, put extra ice in your alcoholic drink to water it down.

☐ Ask a friend to let you know when you have had enough to drink.

☐ Only go out with people you know and trust and make sure you are with people who can take care of you if you drink too much.

☐ Know where your drink has been at all times. Keep it in your hand. If you are at a party, bring your own drink container with a lid. These strategies will help to prevent others from "drugging" your drink.

☐ Use a designated driver or a ride service like Uber.

Go for It!

For the substance use goals that you have chosen to work on first, identify one to three strategies from the aforementioned list that you will try this week.

☐ Check here when you've added them to your calendar or task list.

Module 4.5   Managing Technology Use

College students with ADHD may have more difficulty managing and limiting their technology use than college students without ADHD. Along these lines, Lefler et al. (2022) reported that college students with ADHD tend to engage in more problematic video gaming than college students without ADHD. Although college women engage in lower levels of problematic gaming than college men, college women with ADHD reported more impairment than college men with ADHD as a result of problematic gaming. Problematic gaming in college students with ADHD may result from poor time management and difficulty transitioning from one activity to another. Thus, if gaming (or technology use more generally) is interfering with your academic progress or your social life, you might want to try to determine whether this is a result of difficulty setting limits for yourself once you start gaming and/or using gaming as a way to procrastinate on other tasks.

Benefits of Technology

For those who are trying to optimize their organization, time management, and planning skills (OTMP), technology can be a "double-edged sword". Smartphones provide many useful tools for improving OTMP (e.g., calendars, task lists, reminders, alarms, pomodoro apps). On the other hand, smartphones also provide many tempting distractions (e.g., texting, messaging, social media, gaming). Thus, each time we pick up our phone or get on our computer, we have the potential to be productive or get "sucked in" to something that will impede our productivity. Thus, we have to learn to reap the benefits of technology and resist the temptations. This is hard for all of us regardless of whether we have ADHD.

Maximizing Benefits and Minimizing Problems

The goal, of course, is to maximize the benefits of technology and minimize the problems that it causes for us. Thus, when we get on our phones or computers to check our calendars or task lists, we need to find ways to resist the "black hole" that can result when we check our email, messages, or social media accounts. One way of doing this is to use airplane mode on our phones or turn off the internet on our computers when we are trying to be productive. Other strategies are described here. First, we ask you to assess your technology use and identify any changes that you would like to make. Next, we offer some additional strategies for trying to limit the negative impacts of technology.

Assess Your Technology Use

What Are Your Current Technology Use Habits?

Which of the following do you own?

- ☐ Smartphone
- ☐ Laptop or computer
- ☐ iPad or tablet
- ☐ Gaming system

Which of the following do you engage in?

☐ Texting or messaging (e.g., iMessages, SnapChat)
☐ Social media (e.g., Facebook, Instagram)
☐ YouTube or TikTok videos
☐ Reddit forums
☐ Video or mobile gaming
☐ Television shows or movies (e.g., Netflix, Hulu, Disney+)
☐ Looking at sports sites (e.g., ESPN)

How many hours per day do you think you spend in these activities? (If you are not sure, you can look on your Smartphone or tablet for your daily and weekly screen time data – this can actually be quite enlightening!) _____

Does technology use cause any problems for you like missing class, getting into arguments or fights online, or spending more time or money using technology than you intended?

_____

How satisfied are you with your current habits?

Would you like to make a change?
If so, what change would you like to make?
If yes, why would you like to make a change (e.g., health, academics, relationships)?
How confident are you about your ability to make a change in this area at this time?

Technology Strategies

Which of the Following Strategies Do You Use, Have You Tried, or Would You Be Willing to Try?

☐ Use airplane mode on your phone or turn off the internet on your computer to limit distractions when you are trying to be productive.
☐ Track your screen time using the settings on your phone or an app. Set a goal of reducing use. Reward yourself for progress in this area, perhaps with a fun activity with friends that does not involve technology like playing baseball, going out for coffee, or taking a walk.
☐ Set a limit on the number of minutes or hours you will spend per day engaging in a particular type of technology use (e.g., video gaming). Use phone timers or apps to remind yourself.
☐ Ask your partner, friend, or roommate to set shared goals regarding technology use (e.g., video gaming, Netflix watching) and try to hold each other accountable.
☐ Put your phone in the middle of the table when you are at a restaurant and ask your dining partners to do the same. You can make a game out of it by saying that whoever checks their phone first, must pay the bill.
☐ Make a point to put your phone in another room or in a location where you cannot easily access it (e.g., a drawer) while you are doing school work or spending time with friends or use an app that doesn't allow you to use it while you are doing a Pomodoro (e.g., Forest or Flora).

☐ Carry a book with you so that you can read instead of watching YouTube or checking social media when you have a little down time between activities or have to wait for a class or appointment.

☐ Use technology as a reward for completing other activities (e.g., when I finish this assignment, I will use my phone for 5 minutes; when I finish all my homework, I will play video games for an hour).

Go for It!

For the technology use goals that you have chosen to work on first, identify one to three strategies from the aforementioned list that you will try this week.

☐ Check here when you have put these strategies into your calendar and task list.

Module 4.6   Driving Safely

Research also shows that college students and other adults with ADHD have **impairment related to driving**. Individuals with ADHD have more car accidents, get more speeding tickets, and have more overall driving-related citations than people without ADHD. Those with ADHD also report less use of safe driving behaviors, more risky driving behaviors, more difficulties with concentration while driving, and more instances of anger while driving than individuals without the disorder. In fact, an experimental study compared the simulated driving performance of adults with ADHD and control participants while sober and intoxicated (Weafer et al., 2008). They found that adults with ADHD had poorer driving performance than non-ADHD participants and that **sober adults with ADHD drove as poorly as intoxicated non-ADHD participants** (i.e., blood alcohol level of .08). They concluded that the deficits associated with ADHD may impact driving in the same ways that alcohol impacts driving. Thus, individuals with ADHD should be even more careful about driving under the influence of alcohol (e.g., one drink might be too much) or multitasking while driving (e.g., texting) than those without ADHD.

Another issue is that adults with ADHD may also be prone to overestimating their driving skills and underestimating the impact of alcohol and/or multitasking (Knouse et al., 2005). Currently, we do not have access to driving simulators to test the skill of individual drivers in an objective manner, for instance when they are getting or renewing their driver's license. Thus, we have to rely on adults with ADHD accepting the group data that is available which suggests that adults with ADHD are more likely than adults without ADHD to weave (i.e., drift from their lane), stop and start more quickly, and speed when driving.

Taking stimulant medication consistently as prescribed can reduce these driving-related impairments and risks for those with ADHD (Weafer et al., 2008). However, there are limitations to the use of ADHD medications including that they do not work for everyone, many college students with ADHD do not take them consistently, and the effects have typically worn off by evening which is a time when many emerging adults do a lot of driving. Thus, other behavioral strategies that may help reduce driving risks in those with ADHD are described here.

Assess Your Driving

Do you drive? What is your driving like?

Have you gotten any tickets or citations?

Do you tend to speed while driving?

Do you text and drive? Do you change your music while you are driving?

Are you often distracted while driving?

Have you been in any accidents, or had "near-misses?"

Do your friends and/or significant other complain about your driving?

How satisfied are you with your current habits?

Would you like to make any changes to your driving?

    If so, what kind of changes would you like to make?
    If so, why would you like to make a change (e.g., health, legal repercussions, relationships)?
    How confident are you about your ability to make a change in this area at this time?

Safe Driving Strategies

Which of the Following Strategies Do You Use, Have You Tried, or Would You Be Willing to Try?

☐ If you take stimulant medicine for your **ADHD**, take it regularly at the scheduled time. You will be a more attentive driver if you are taking your medication as prescribed.

☐ Set your phone to automatically go to do-not-disturb when you are driving. Leave your phone in the backseat or trunk while you are driving.

☐ Adjust your music or look up driving directions before you begin a drive, not during the drive.

☐ Schedule long driving trips early in the day when you are rested and alert. Take a break every 2 hours.

☐ Ask a friend or family member to join you on long driving trips.

☐ Let your passenger be in charge of driving directions and/or music while you are driving even if it takes them longer to find the directions or the song than it would take you.

☐ If you are comfortable, let your passenger read your texts and respond for you while you are driving.

☐ Limit the number of passengers that you take in your car to reduce distractions while driving (e.g., driving five drunk friends to a party may be very distracting).

☐ Make a commitment not to drive after drinking or using drugs.

☐ Consider taking a taxi, Uber, or Lyft (or public transportation if available) instead of driving if there is a large group or anyone has been drinking or using drugs (if these services are not available where you live, call a friend or family member).

Go for It!

For the driving goals that you have chosen to work on first, identify one to three strategies from the aforementioned list that you will try this week.

☐ Check here when you've put them in your calendar or task list.

Note

1 If there are very few healthy foods you like to eat, this is something you can work on! If this is a problem for you, we recommend setting up an appointment with a nutritionist or counselor to discuss strategies for expanding your diet.

References

Hillman, C. H., Erickson, K. I., & Kramer, A. F. (2008). Be smart, exercise your heart: Exercise effects on brain and cognition. *Nature Reviews Neuroscience, 9*(1), 58–65. https://doi.org/10.1038/nrn2298

Hoover, D. W., & Milich, R. (1994). Effects of sugar ingestion expectancies on mother-child interactions. *Journal of Abnormal Child Psychology, 22*(4), 501–515. https://doi.org/10.1007/BF02168088

Knouse, L. E., Bagwell, C. L., Barkley, R. A., & Murphy, K. R. (2005). Accuracy of self-evaluation in adults with ADHD: Evidence from a driving study. *Journal of Attention Disorders, 8*, 221–234.

Kuntsche, E., Knibbe, R., Gmel, G., & Engels, R. (2005). Why do young people drink? A review of drinking motives. *Clinical Psychology Review, 25*(7), 841–861. https://doi.org/10.1016/j.cpr.2005.06.002

LaCount, P. A., Hartung, C. M., Vasko, J. M., Serrano, J. W., Wright, H. A., & Smith, D. T. (2022). Acute effects of physical exercise on cognitive and psychological functioning in college students with attention-deficit/hyperactivity disorder. *Mental Health and Physical Activity, 22*, 100443. https://doi.org/10.1016/j.mhpa.2022.100443

Lefler, E. K., Alacha, H. F., Vasko, J. M, Serrano, J. W., Looby, A., Flory, K., & Hartung, C. M. (2022 in press). Sex differences in ADHD symptoms, problematic gaming, and impairment in college students. *Current Psychology*.

Looby, A., Prince, M. A., Vasko, J. M., Zimmerman, L., Lefler, E. K., Flory, K., Canu, W., & Hartung, C. M. (2021). Relations among protective behavioral strategies, biological sex, and ADHD symptoms on alcohol use and related problems: Who benefits most, and from what type of strategy? *Addictive Behaviors, 119*, 106924. https://doi.org/10.1016/j.addbeh.2021.106924

Nigg, J. T. (2018). *Getting ahead of ADHD: What next-generation science says about treatments that work – and how you can make them work for your child* (pp. vii, 299). Guilford Press.

Rebar, A. L., Stanton, R., Geard, D., Short, C., Duncan, M. J., & Vandelanotte, C. (2015). A meta-meta-analysis of the effect of physical activity on depression and anxiety in non-clinical adult populations. *Health Psychology Review, 9*(3), 366–378. https://doi.org/10.1080/17437199.2015.1022901

Tsai, H.-J., Yang, A. C., Zhu, J.-D., Hsu, Y.-Y., Hsu, T.-F., & Tsai, S.-J. (2022). Effectiveness of digital cognitive behavioral therapy for insomnia in young people: Preliminary findings from systematic review and meta-analysis. *Journal of Personalized Medicine*, *12*(3), 481. https://doi.org/10.3390/jpm12030481

U.S. Department of Health and Human Services. (2018). *Physical Activity Guidelines for Americans* (2nd ed., p. 118). U.S. Department of Health and Human Services.

Wajszilber, D., Santiseban, J. A., & Gruber, R. (2018). Sleep disorders in patients with ADHD: Impact and management challenges. *Nature and Science of Sleep*, *10*, 453–480. https://doi.org/10.2147/NSS.S163074

Weafer, J., Camarillo, D., Fillmore, M. T., Milich, R., & Marczinski, C. A. (2008). Simulated driving performance of adults with ADHD: Comparisons with alcohol intoxication. *Experimental and Clinical Psychopharmacology*, *16*(3), 251–263.

5 Building Strong Relationships

Module 5.0 Why It Matters and Roadmap

While it certainly isn't the case for all people with ADHD, research has shown that many – perhaps half – have social difficulties. Whether the relationship troubles are with childhood peers, teachers, family members, or romantic interests or partners, it seems like basically across the board the risk for rejection or impairment is higher for those with ADHD than for others. As you think back on your life, you may nod along as you read this . . . or, maybe, you won't, because for you it wasn't that hard. Either way, but especially if this topic feels "fresh" to you (as in "yeah, I have problems in my relationships *now!*"), we recommend you to at least consider learning or at least brushing up on some effective relationship skills – and how ADHD can get in the way of these.

Our focus in this skillset is on two broad types of relationships that, in our experience, can be difficult for college students with ADHD: those with one's peers (friends, romantic partners), and those with one's parents. Of course, these can be stressful or unsatisfying for various reasons, but both are also important for most people in their lives. While some skills and perspectives are versatile and apply to both types of relationships, others are more specific. In any event, now it's time to. . .

 Check Yourself: Which Relationships Need Attention?

Complete the checklist to help you figure out which modules in this chapter may be most helpful for you.

Self-Assessment of Relationships. Complete the following worksheet, based on how these apply to you on a day-to-day basis in recent memory (about the last six months). Circle one response per item, using this scale: **0 = Never, 1 = Sometimes, 2 = Often, 3 = Very Often**.

1. I have trouble getting along with my peers.   0   1   2   3

2. I have arguments with friends or intimate partners.   0   1   2   3

DOI: 10.4324/9781003149620-6

3.	I have trouble starting new relationships with friends or intimate partners.	0	1	2	3
4.	I have trouble maintaining friendships or intimate relationships.	0	1	2	3
5.	I have trouble getting what I need from friends or intimate partners.	0	1	2	3
6.	I say or do things I later regret to friends or intimate partners.	0	1	2	3
7.	I wish that my relationships with friends or intimate partners could be better.	0	1	2	3
8.	I have conflicts or arguments with my parents.	0	1	2	3
9.	I get the feeling that my parents don't trust me.	0	1	2	3
10.	My parents are too involved in my life.	0	1	2	3
11.	My parents don't provide me with the support I think I need.	0	1	2	3
12.	I wish that my relationship with my parents could be better.	0	1	2	3
13.	I wish communications with my parents could be better.	0	1	2	3

Make Your Plan

1. **Choose modules** based on the following and check them off in your plan here:

   Questions 1–7: If you marked more than one item "2" or "3", include **Module 5.1**.
   Questions 8–13: If you marked more than one item "2" or "3", include **Module 5.2**.

2. **Work on the modules** you selected in the order that they appear by adding each module to your **task list and/or calendar** and tackling them one at a time. Check off each module when you finish it and **reward yourself for a job well done**!

Relationship Skills Plan

In my plan?	Done	Module		Pages
		Module 5.1. *Improve Relationships with Friends and Partners*		**117–127**
		Module 5.2. *Navigate Your Relationships with Parents*		**127–137**

Module 5.1   Improve Relationships With Friends and Partners

If you're reading this, it's because you've thought about your social experience and realize that it's not infrequent that your friendships and/or romantic relationships are at least a little rocky. That, by itself, is really not that unusual. Relationships are tough! It takes flexibility, empathy, caring, and dedication . . . at a minimum, and that's when other things like personality and interests are fairly well matched. This means that relationships are, in a word, *work*. Of course, they can also be satisfying and sources of real support, too. A key thing for college students with ADHD to maximize these types of outcomes, versus rejection or unhappiness, is understanding how their specific deficits impact them socially and developing the "right" set of skills to succeed. There's no time like the present to start learning these things!

Knowing Yourself: How Does ADHD Affect Me in Relationships?

As noted earlier, relationships are work . . . and every relationship with someone else is unique, too. You first have to learn what it means to be a good friend, what it means to be a good romantic partner (if that's something you're interested in) . . . and *then* you have to adapt to the needs and interests of the specific people you choose to be your friends or your partners. If you have worked with or are currently seeing a therapist to help you live your best life, or if you've just done some reading on your own about ADHD, or if you've even reflected on your own experiences at some point, you likely have realized that certain things about this disorder can complicate this process of being in relationships and even just interacting with others, like:

- **Inattention/Loss of focus:** problems like failing to notice it's time to meet someone, or zoning out in a conversation, or losing something important to someone else
- **Impulsivity:** problems like committing to things you end up not wanting to do, or saying something totally not the way you wanted, or not following "the rules"
- **Emotional dysregulation:** problems like overreacting to situations, really quickly getting angry or upset and having a hard time controlling it

So, naturally, you may have bigger challenges than someone who doesn't have ADHD when it comes to having and keeping good relationships. Take a second, and reflect on this now by answering the following questions.

Are relationships difficult for you? If so, what types, and how?

_____

_____

_____

_____

How do you think your ADHD relates to this?

_____

_____

_____

_____

Now, let's dig down even a little bit deeper . . . complete the following forms, which will give you some more info about your own relationship behaviors that can be pretty important to "going the distance". Note that if you have not been in a serious (i.e., beyond just physical) romantic relationship, the Conflict Resolution Inventory may not yet be for you . . . you can always come back and fill that out later if it starts to apply!

Interpersonal Competence Questionnaire

Rate how good you think you are at the following relationships tasks, and then calculate the total score for each section where indicated.

	I'm poor at this	*I'm only fair at this*	*I'm okay at this*	*I'm good at this*	*I'm extremely good at this*
Asking or suggesting to someone new that you get together and do something, e.g., go out together.	1	2	3	4	5
Finding and suggesting things to do with new people whom you find interesting and attractive.	1	2	3	4	5
Carrying on conversations with someone new whom you think you might like to get to know.	1	2	3	4	5
Being an interesting and enjoyable person to be with when first getting to know people.	1	2	3	4	5
Calling (on the phone) a new date/acquaintance to set up a time to get together and do something.	1	2	3	4	5
Telling a companion that they have done something to hurt your feelings.	1	2	3	4	5
Going to parties or gatherings where you don't know people well in order to start up new relationships.	1	2	3	4	5

TOTAL (add values from each item) **Initiating Relationships =**

	I'm poor at this	*I'm only fair at this*	*I'm okay at this*	*I'm good at this*	*I'm extremely good at this*
Revealing something intimate about yourself while talking with someone you're just getting to know.	1	2	3	4	5
Confiding in a new friend/date and letting them see your softer, more sensitive side.	1	2	3	4	5
Telling a close companion things about yourself that you're ashamed of.	1	2	3	4	5
Letting a new companion get to know the "real you".	1	2	3	4	5
Letting down your protective "outer shell" and trusting a close companion.	1	2	3	4	5
Telling a close companion about the things that secretly make you feel anxious or afraid.	1	2	3	4	5
Telling a close companion how much you appreciate and care for them.	1	2	3	4	5
Knowing how to move a conversation with a date/acquaintance beyond superficial talk to really get to know each other.	1	2	3	4	5

TOTAL: Self-Disclosure =

	I'm poor at this	*I'm only fair at this*	*I'm okay at this*	*I'm good at this*	*I'm extremely good at this*
Telling a companion you don't like a certain way they have been treating you.	1	2	3	4	5

(*Continued*)

	I'm poor at this	I'm only fair at this	I'm okay at this	I'm good at this	I'm extremely good at this
Saying "no" when a date/acquaintance asks you to do something you don't want to do.	1	2	3	4	5
Turning down a request by a companion that is unreasonable.	1	2	3	4	5
Standing up for your rights when a companion is neglecting you or being inconsiderate.	1	2	3	4	5
Telling a date/acquaintance that they are doing something that embarrasses you.	1	2	3	4	5
Confronting your close companion when they have broken a promise.	1	2	3	4	5
Telling a date/acquaintance that they have done something that made you angry.	1	2	3	4	5

TOTAL: Asserting Displeasure with Others' Actions =

	I'm poor at this	I'm only fair at this	I'm okay at this	I'm good at this	I'm extremely good at this
Helping a close companion work through their thoughts and feelings about a major life decision, e.g., a career choice.	1	2	3	4	5
Being able to patiently and sensitively listen to a companion "let off steam" about outside problems they are having.	1	2	3	4	5
Helping a close companion get to the heart of a problem they are experiencing.	1	2	3	4	5
Helping a close companion cope with family or roommate problems.	1	2	3	4	5
Being a good and sensitive listener for a companion who is upset.	1	2	3	4	5
Being able to say and do things to support a close companion when they are feeling down.	1	2	3	4	5
Being able to show genuine empathetic concern even when a companion's problem is uninteresting to you.	1	2	3	4	5
When a close companion needs help and support, being able to give advice in ways that are well received.	1	2	3	4	5

TOTAL SCORE: Providing Emotional Support =

	I'm poor at this	I'm only fair at this	I'm okay at this	I'm good at this	I'm extremely good at this
Being able to admit that you might be wrong when a disagreement with a close companion begins to build into a serious fight.	1	2	3	4	5
Being able to put begrudging (resentful) feelings aside when having a fight with a close companion.	1	2	3	4	5

	I'm poor at this	I'm only fair at this	I'm okay at this	I'm good at this	I'm extremely good at this
When having a conflict with a close companion, really listening to their complaints and not trying to "read" their mind.	1	2	3	4	5
Being able to take a companion's perspective in a fight and really understand their point of view.	1	2	3	4	5
Refraining from saying things that might cause a disagreement to build into a big fight.	1	2	3	4	5
Being able to work through a specific problem with a companion without resorting to global accusations ("you always do that").	1	2	3	4	5
When angry with a companion, being able to accept that they have a valid point of view even if you don't agree with that view.	1	2	3	4	5
Not exploding at a close companion (even when it is justified) in order to avoid a damaging conflict.	1	2	3	4	5

TOTAL SCORE: Managing Interpersonal Conflicts =

Conflict Resolution Inventory

Rate <u>how frequently you use each of the following styles to deal with arguments or disagreements</u> with your partner. Then calculate the total score for each section where indicated.

	Never ------------------> Always				
Launching personal attacks	1	2	3	4	5
Exploding and getting out of control	1	2	3	4	5
Getting carried away and saying things that aren't meant	1	2	3	4	5
Throwing insults and digs	1	2	3	4	5
TOTAL SCORE: Conflict Engagement (sum of items) =					
Not being willing to stick up for myself	1	2	3	4	5
Being too compliant	1	2	3	4	5
Not defending my position	1	2	3	4	5
Giving in with little attempt to present my side of the issue	1	2	3	4	5
TOTAL SCORE: Compliance =					

(Continued)

	Never – ------------------> Always				
Remaining silent for long periods of time	1	2	3	4	5
Reaching a limit, "shutting down", and refusing to talk any further	1	2	3	4	5
Tuning the other person out	1	2	3	4	5
Withdrawing, acting distance and not interested	1	2	3	4	5
TOTAL SCORE: Withdrawal =					
Focusing on the problem at hand	1	2	3	4	5
Sitting down and discussing differences constructively	1	2	3	4	5
Finding alternatives that are acceptable to each of us	1	2	3	4	5
Negotiating and compromising	1	2	3	4	5
TOTAL SCORE: Positive Problem Solving =					

Now let's consider what your answers to all those questions suggest about your interpersonal style. First, make sure you have calculated your scores on the measures. The Interpersonal Competence Questionnaire has five scales, with scores between 1 ("I'm poor at this") and 5 ("I'm extremely good at this") on each. These scales basically indicate your relative strength in skills like getting the ball rolling in social situations and relationships (**Initiating Relationships**), comfort with opening up to someone else (**Self-Disclosure**), expressing your opinion or needs even when it involves some degree of confrontation (**Asserting Displeasure with Others' Actions**), having empathy for and being able to effectively, emotionally support others (**Providing Emotional Support**), and being able to work through conflict in social situations without damaging relationships (**Managing Interpersonal Conflicts**).

The Conflict Resolution Inventory is more specific, focusing in more depth on a skill that is really important for the success of romantic relationships. It documents how often you employ different conflict strategies using four scales, with a familiar 1 ("Never") to 5 ("Always") score on each. **Conflict engagement** really is about behaviors that tend to intensify conflict – the proverbial gasoline on the fire! **Compliance**, or just going along with your partner's opinions or desires to resolve the situation, and **Withdrawal**, or basically shutting down during conflict, are neutral in comparison but can also feel bad, postpone solutions, or make matters worse. **Positive problem solving**, on the other hand, involves in engaging in behaviors that may be hard and even uncomfortable but that ultimately lead to agreements and compromises that can be mutually acceptable.

So, what do you notice from your results? Take a second to write about it here.

What sorts of relational strengths do you bring to the table?

_____

_____

_____

_____

What are your relative weaknesses in relationships?

_____

_____

_____

_____

Things like impulsivity and inattention can play a role in relationships. Do you think your ADHD relates to either strengths or weaknesses? How?

_____

_____

_____

_____

What Do I Need to Do to Be Successful in My Relationships?

One of the things that you may be already realizing is that there are some skills that are simply important to having steady and satisfying relationships. The following are some of the most important ones that relate to what you've just been finding out about yourself.

1. *Positive Conflict Resolution*

This means having conversation about the conflict but keeping focused on understanding each other's perspectives and potential solutions. Withdrawal from the conflict without follow-up really represents a failure to address the problem, and it may just fester and get worse. Equally important is avoiding excessive or harsh criticism and any physical aggression. However, staying cool-headed and focused on resolving conflict can be hard when you have ADHD! Knowing when you are at the "boiling point" and then being able to implement self-soothing or physical distancing is a necessary skill. Some ideas here include:

- *"Take Five"*. Ask for a few minutes to cool off when you notice you are getting hot, before you say something you will regret.
- *Think It Through*. What is happening? What are you arguing about? What is the actual problem here, and what are some ways to solve it?
- *Take a Note*. Instead of immediately saying what is bothering you, write it down. This can be something useful to do when you are Taking Five that helps you to Think it Through better.
- *Plan What You Say*. This is where open communication comes in.

If acting impulsively during relationship conflicts is a significant problem for you, you may also want to check out Skillset 3, specifically **Module 3.4** on Impulsive Emotions.

2. Open (and Tactful!) Communication

This is basically behaving in a *direct and positive* way, which is really important to effectively resolve conflicts. If your ADHD involves mainly difficulty with attention (and less hyperactivity and impulsivity), it is possible that you may recognize having particular difficulty with this. Furthermore, while being able to articulate your perspectives and views, wants and needs is really important, it is equally important that the message does not come across like a bomb! For example, "You are just the worst! I can't believe you are ignoring me and just looking at that stupid device!" is likely to be hurtful, whereas "Are you doing something important now? I really like it when it's just us two and we can talk together, and I was hoping we could do that now" is softer and still requests the change.

Some suggest that the use of "**I-messages**" is a good framework for direct communication of potentially tough messages. These

- *communicate your feeling,*
- *specify the "problem", and*
- *invite discussion or offer a suggestion.*

So, in the aforementioned situation, an I-message would be something like "I feel frustrated now, when you are on your iPhone and we haven't seen each other all day. Is it possible for us to put aside our devices for half-an-hour when we get together?"

3. Being a Good Listener

Good listeners pay attention to their conversation partners, and to the content and flow of what they're talking about. It is often possible to *see* this, as a good listener may lean toward the other person, naturally match their tone to that of the partner, nod at appropriate times, and so on. Good listeners also do things like ask questions that relate to what a person has just said, and say empathic things like "that seems like it's hard for you" when it's called for. Again, this may be naturally hard for you; if your mind is wandering, or you impulsively interrupt or change subjects abruptly, it can lead to hurt feelings or frustration on the part of your friend or partner, and a disconnect in your relationship.

Becoming a better listener will take a conscious effort. A few things that you can do to start building this skill are:

- *Show them you are listening.* At a pause when a friend is talking with you, try addressing the point your friend just made, but with your own words and perspective. So, if they said "I can't believe my professor asked us to do this on such short notice!", you might respond "yeah, that would totally take me off guard, too".
- *Check the tone.* When you're having a conversation with someone, try to tune in beyond the words . . . what is the feeling that the person is conveying? Recognizing quickly that someone is upset or stoked about something can help you to tune in on an emotional level, and you can show them you notice and care with a quick response ("I'm so sorry", "That is awesome!").

Sometimes, doing things like this may seem a little forced (e.g., "You mean I have to repeat back what someone says to me?"), but in the end it will help friends and partners to feel more understood – really important for emotional support – and will help you better connect with others.

4. Reciprocate!

How does it feel to you when a conversation seems entirely one-sided? When a friend dictates the topics, or seems to just want to talk about themselves? This gets back to being a good listener: That is impossible when you are doing *all* of the talking! Taking turns is key (e.g., "So that was my day . . . how was yours?"). It is also usually very appreciated when someone actively asks the opinion or thoughts of others (e.g., "Does that fit with your schedule tonight?"). Reciprocity can also be thought of as giving back what you get in a relationship. For example, if a friend takes several hours to help repair your car, it makes sense that when that friend needs help with some similarly onerous task that you should step up. One easy way to think about reciprocity is to invoke the proverbial "Golden Rule" – do for others what you want them to do for you! In relationships, burdens are best shared, instead of being shouldered by only one partner (or friend).

- *Start slow.* Basically, make it not all about you from the get-go. Make a point to check in with your friend about their day, or about something you talked about the last time.
- *Check yourself, and check in with others.* Make a mental note: Have I just been talking for a long time? Have I talked a lot about something without checking what my friend thinks? If so, switch gears! Say "Oh, well, enough about me, what's up with you?" or ask "Hey, so I'm wondering what you think about all that?" or something like that which says "I want to know your perspective".
- *Feel the room.* Is your friend expressing any negative feelings? Notice them, out loud (e.g., "Dude, I'm sorry, I'd be [angry, sad, stressed] too"). Or is your friend expressing a need for help? If you can, offer it (e.g., "hey, I may not be an expert at that, but if you need a hand I think I can make some time!").
- *Get confirmations.* Sometimes we can talk so much about something, and maybe really enthusiastically, and a friend may be nodding along but still thinking about it. So if you think you've agreed on something, check in anyway (e.g., "So, does it fit for you to see that movie on Friday?").

5. Notice and Respond to Others' Needs

This can be easier said than done, depending on who you're with. However, the point here is that it can be easy to forget the desires and needs of friends or partners when you're interacting, maybe especially so in a group situation. Some examples of how this might come up include:

- You know your partner is introverted, so at a party it makes sense to tune into how engaged and energized they are (e.g., privately say "Hey, seems like you're getting tired . . . you wanna go in a few minutes?").
- Your friend has just texted that they're sick and in bed. Offer to bring a meal, or pick up other things they need.
- Your partner just got home after a really long day at school. Don't push them to go out and do errands with you right away; ask if they need some time to relax first or if it's best for you to take care of it.

While this set of action items does not necessarily cover *all* the bases when it comes to success and happiness in relationships, we think these are critical skills, and ones that college students with

ADHD may have particular deficits in. So, now . . . time to practice, practice, practice, and see how it goes!

What skills and behaviors noted earlier do you want to work on?

_____

_____

_____

_____

How and with whom do you think you can practice those skills?

_____

_____

_____

_____

OK!! Now, **make a commitment to yourself to begin doing these things**!

☐ **Check here when you've written your plans in your calendar or task list.**

You may also want to tell trusted others you are working on this . . . they may give you encouraging and other helpful feedback! Something that will help to motivate you even more is to track what you are doing. On the next page, we have included a journal worksheet for you that focuses on behaviors and how you think they work in your friendships and/or romantic relationships. We recommend that you complete this once a day for a week, capturing the results of the things you are choosing to work on. We bet that after that week you will see positive results, enough that we hope you will make your new skills part of your everyday routine. When you've completed the week, think about giving yourself a little reward to reinforce your efforts, too!

Situation	Skill Practiced	How did it go?	What did you learn?

Situation	Skill Practiced	How did it go?	What did you learn?

 There are good resources out there that can help explain the sorts of skills that we have discussed in this chapter. Here are some that you might find helpful.

Web

Conflict Resolution: How to Settle Your Differences Fairly | BrainPOP www.youtube.com/watch?v=jg_Q34kGsKg

Reading

Pollack, J. (2020). *Conflict Resolution Playbook: Practical Communication Skills for Preventing, Managing, and Resolving Conflict.* Rockridge Press. Available at Amazon.com

Module 5.2   Navigate Your Relationships With Parents

One or both of your parents might be your most active champions and supporters. They may have coached you through elementary, middle, and high school, helping with added structure and clear expectations, providing extra reinforcement when you accomplished hard things, providing encouragement and a shoulder to lean on when you needed it. But the research on families with children with ADHD also suggests that many parents and their kids have strained relationships. Parents may not fully understand ADHD, and even if they do they may be frustrated a lot with their kid's behavior, or just feel tired of trying to "fix" things when ADHD gets in the way. So anger, exasperation, blame, and criticism can seep into the relationship, and parents may be overly strict and punitive, making it feel kind of toxic (this is sometimes referred to as *authoritarian* parenting). On the other hand, parents may just kind of throw their hands up and instead of engaging and supporting, simply let their kid with ADHD make all the choices, and basically do whatever they want (this is called *permissive* parenting). These styles contrast with *authoritative* parenting, where parents not only have clear expectations and standards but also explain their reasoning and take their children's perspectives and emotions into account. If you are curious about the type of parenting you tended to get most, you can complete the questionnaire that follows.

For each of the following statements, circle the number that best describes how that statement applies to you and your parents. Try to read and think about each statement as it applies to you and your parents during your years of growing up at home. If your answers differ for each parent, you can choose different answers for each.

	Strongly Disagree	*Disagree*	*Neither Agree nor Disagree*	*Agree*	*Strongly Agree*
While I was growing up, my parents felt that, in a well-run home, the children should have their way in the family as often as the parents do.	1	2	3	4	5
My parents have always felt that what their children need is to be free to make up their own minds and to do what they want to do, even if this does not agree with what their parents might want.	1	2	3	4	5
As I was growing up my parents did not feel that I needed to obey rules and regulations of behavior simply because someone in authority had established them.	1	2	3	4	5
As I was growing up, my parents seldom gave me expectations and guidelines for my behavior.	1	2	3	4	5
Most of the time as I was growing up my parents did what the children in the family wanted when making family decisions.	1	2	3	4	5
My parents feel that most problems in society would be solved if parents would not restrict their children's activities, decisions, and desires as they are growing up.	1	2	3	4	5
As I was growing up my parents allowed me to decide most things for myself without a lot of direction from them.	1	2	3	4	5
My parents did not view themselves as responsible for directing and guiding my behavior as I was growing up.	1	2	3	4	5
As I was growing up my parents allowed me to form my own point of view on family matters and they generally allowed me to decide for myself what I was going to do.	1	2	3	4	5

	Strongly Disagree	Disagree	Neither Agree nor Disagree	Agree	Strongly Agree
As I was growing up my parents did not direct the behaviors, activities, and desires of the children in the family.	1	2	3	4	5

Total Permissive Parenting (add all columns) =

	Strongly Disagree	Disagree	Neither Agree nor Disagree	Agree	Strongly Agree
Even if their children didn't agree with them, my parents felt that it was for our own good if we were forced to conform to what they thought was right.	1	2	3	4	5
Whenever my parents told me to do something as I was growing up, they expected me to do it immediately without asking any questions.	1	2	3	4	5
As I was growing up my parents did not allow me to question any decision they had made.	1	2	3	4	5
My parents have always felt that more force should be used by parents in order to get their children to behave the way they are supposed to.	1	2	3	4	5
My parents felt that wise parents should teach their children early just who is boss in the family.	1	2	3	4	5
As I was growing up my parents would get very upset if I tried to disagree with them.	1	2	3	4	5
As I was growing up my parents let me know what behavior they expected of me, and if I didn't meet those expectations, they punished me.	1	2	3	4	5
My parents have always felt that most problems in society would be solved if we could get parents to strictly and forcibly deal with their children when they don't do what they are supposed to as they are growing up.	1	2	3	4	5
As I was growing up my parents often told me exactly what they wanted me to do and how they expected me to do it.	1	2	3	4	5
As I was growing up I knew what my parents expected of me in the family and they insisted that I conform to those expectations simply out of respect for their authority.	1	2	3	4	5

Total Authoritarian Parenting =

(Continued)

	Strongly Disagree	Disagree	Neither Agree nor Disagree	Agree	Strongly Agree
As I was growing up, once family policy had been established, my parents discussed the reasoning behind the policy with the children in the family.	1	2	3	4	5
My parents have always encouraged verbal give-and-take whenever I have felt that family rules and restrictions were unreasonable.	1	2	3	4	5
As I was growing up my parents directed the activities and decisions of the children in the family through reasoning and discipline.	1	2	3	4	5
As I was growing up I knew what my parents expected of me in my family, but I also felt free to discuss those expectations with them when I felt that they were unreasonable.	1	2	3	4	5
As the children in my family were growing up, my parents consistently gave us direction and guidance in rational and objective ways.	1	2	3	4	5
As I was growing up, my parents took the children's opinions into consideration when making family decisions, but they would not decide on something simply because the children wanted it.	1	2	3	4	5
My parents had clear standards of behavior for the children in our home as I was growing up, but they were willing to adjust those standards to the needs of each of the individual children in the family.	1	2	3	4	5
My parents gave me direction for my behavior and activities as I was growing up and they expected me to follow their direction, but they were always willing to listen to my concerns and to discuss that direction with me.	1	2	3	4	5
As I was growing up my parents gave me clear direction for my behaviors and activities, but they were also understanding when I disagreed with them.	1	2	3	4	5
As I was growing up, if my parents made a decision in the family that hurt me, they were willing to discuss that decision with me and to admit it if they had made a mistake.	1	2	3	4	5

Total Score Authoritative Parenting =

Whether your relationship with your parents was generally supportive or conflicted in some way, your transition to college and to adulthood, in general, changes the game. You are "in charge" now. You may not even be living at home anymore, and the amount of contact you have with your parents may be relatively limited. College is an important time to learn how to care for yourself and take charge of your life – "adulting", in other words. But this can be hard, especially when you're new to it.

Let's consider an analogy for getting through college and "emerging" adulthood", which is what psychologists call the time period from about 18–29 years old: learning to be a pilot. No one gets into a cockpit for the first time and knows how to fly the plane. First, you take introductory lessons and learn in ground school. Then, with an instructor, you do a lot of practice in a single-engine propeller plane. You pass a test, then graduate, and can fly single-engine propeller planes on your own, in the daytime. If you want to be a commercial pilot, you then have to take additional courses and have practice flying with instruments instead of visual cues, multi-engine propeller planes, small jets, and then the big ones like the airlines have. This process takes thousands of hours of work . . . and, importantly, **a lot of practice and help along the way**.

So, in other words, even though it might be annoying at times, **you may still need some support and advice from your parents** (assuming your relationship is not totally defined by toxicity), even though your situation has changed a lot from being at home in high school to now being in college. At the same time, **you can't learn to fly the plane if your parents are always in the pilot's seat**. In other words, you need to begin to take on more responsibility while still taking advantage of support when needed. The million dollar question is, though: How can I negotiate a relationship with my parents that recognizes I'm an adult, provides just the help that I still need, and is also a happy and satisfying experience, for all of us?

 Let's take stock of your specific experience and perspective on a few things now that will help you to do this!

Since you have started college, what sorts of *problems* have emerged in your relationship with your parents (i.e., what do they do that annoys you?)

_____

_____

_____

_____

_____

_____

To be fair: Since you have started college, what sorts of *benefits* have emerged in those relationships (i.e., what are they doing that you really appreciate)?

_____

_____

Any other thoughts you have about your current relationships with your parents?

Alright, that's a lot to consider! Maybe some things came up for you that were really positive, maybe some things that were pretty negative. Maybe you feel like giving your parents a call right now! Well, hang on just a bit . . . we'll get to that later. Hopefully, at least there is some mixture of things that you appreciate that they do along with other things that you could really do without. There are a couple of important principles, then, to keep in mind as you consolidate a new understanding and relationship with your parents that best fits you now as a college student. The first, perhaps obviously, is that you want to *keep the positive, and cut back on the negative*. The second, and this is something that was also really emphasized in **Module 5.1**, is to remember that *your relationship with your parent(s) is a two-way street*.

Negotiating Your New and Improved Relationship

First, we would be remiss if we didn't put in a plug for the kinds of relationship skills that we presented in Module 5.1. While you might be reading this and have chosen to do this module and not the last one given how your friendships are (i.e., you're doing well with those), there are some really important ideas and skills in Module 5.1 that are just as important in your relationship with your parents. So, we recommend reading and/or reviewing that material, and practicing it with your parents.

Next, let's talk more about keeping the positive and cutting back on the negative. This will be crucial for "The Big Talk" that you will want to have with your parents to move your relationships to this new level: adult parent with adult child *who still has some needs that the parent can help with*. Take a look at what you wrote earlier about problems and benefits (and other reflections) about your current relationship with your parents. Consider these questions:

- What is the relative balance between problems and benefits? If the benefits you note are clearly outweighing the problems, both in number and importance, good for you! This is an enviable position; your Big Talk can include a lot of reinforcement of what your parents are "doing right" and it's likely that they will be receptive to your request for change in the other area(s).

- If there are roughly the same number of problems and benefits, that's fine, too; one communication strategy that is often referenced is to "sandwich" the negative with positives. An example of a "Benefit Sandwich" would be to:

  - open with thanking your parents for their supportive weekly check-in calls (benefit),
  - switch to discussing Dad's daily texts asking about current and new assignments and grades in classes (problem) and Mom's contact with your roommate's parents about their pattern of having overnight guests (problem), and then
  - reiterating your appreciation for your parents helping to make your goals a reality with their financial support (benefit).

- If the problems on your list clearly outweigh the positives, in order for your initial relationship renegotiation to work in your favor, we recommend prioritizing your "asks" (the problems you discuss) and bringing only as many asks to the table as you do honest benefits. The thing to realize in this case is that relationships are dynamic, and morph over time. A little change on the important things now may actually help your chance of having a really good relationship with your parent(s) in the future. So, (a) prioritize the problems, (b) take the top ones (as many as you have benefits to reinforce), and (c) then make a Benefit Sandwich, like described earlier.

OK, now, take a second to note:

Considering my balance of problems and benefits in my relationship with my parents, how should my strategy look when talking with them?

_____

_____

_____

_____

_____

_____

It's Not Really All About Me

Now, let's put the "relationship shoe" on the other foot, so to speak. We have found that in our clinical practice, whether working with parents, kids, college students, teachers, or others, one of the key points in effective communication and collaboration is *understanding*. By working to understand someone else's story, their point of view, we develop empathy for what that person is going through and dealing with, and engaging from that stance goes a long way to finding mutually acceptable solutions to problems and also to building good will.

Parents can experience a lot of different thoughts and emotions when their adult child goes to college, depending on a lot of different things about their life. Some may experience their child's departure as a real loss, which at least at first causes real sadness, maybe out of loneliness or loss of perceived purpose or sudden change in personal connection. Parents who provided a lot of support to their child in high school and earlier may be pretty worried about whether their child can cope with the rigors of college. They may perceive it as a dangerous time: Maybe their child will be hurt by someone (physically or emotionally), maybe their child will fail and become despondent or hopeless, maybe their child's opinions or personality or goals or interests will change so radically that they will become a completely different person, one who does not relate to or appreciate them as they used to. Some parents may even feel jealous or could be confused about what their child is going through, perhaps because they themselves did not attend college or because they did attend and remember it as one of the most exciting and fulfilling times of their lives.

 So, now, it's time to really think about and acknowledge these things:

Given your own history, in your own family, what do you think it's like for your parents now that you are a college student?

_____

_____

_____

_____

_____

_____

Given who your parents are (maybe including what you know from the questionnaire at the beginning of this module), what challenges might they have in changing the way they relate to you, now?

_____

_____

_____

_____

_____

_____

Given these thoughts about your parents' perspective(s), do you have any new thoughts about your relationship and your situation? Is there anything that you think you should talk with them about, or acknowledge to them, that could make renegotiating your relationship easier or more effective?

_____

_____

_____

_____

_____

_____

The Big Talk

You have done a lot of thinking about your relationship with your parents now, and have a grasp on what your needs are (problems to resolve), what you appreciate about their current parenting (benefits to acknowledge), some idea about how to communicate the relative balance of those things, and a better understanding of their perspective in all of this. Now, it's time for the final step . . . starting the change process, by having your Big Talk.

The first step is to figure out a good time to do this. Ideally, you should choose a time when you can do this in private (i.e., not at a restaurant or at the Thanksgiving dinner table with other family members) and neither you nor your parents are in a hurry, stressed out, or have other big things on the agenda. In other words, minimizing distractions and also "baseline" agitation will improve the chances that this goes well. (In fact, this is a good general tip for successful negotiation.) So. . .

When and where do you want to plan to have this conversation with your parent(s)?

_____

_____

The next very concrete step is to simply ask your parents if this is a good time to do this, and also tell them the purpose. Nobody likes to be ambushed by a conversation that could feel a little difficult (e.g., parents may have a hard time discussing their own behavior with their child), so this is important. You do not have to have the whole conversation to tell them about it; you can simply say something like "I was hoping that we could talk a bit about how things are going for me in college and the ways that you can help me to do well. Is [your proposed time] good for you guys?" We definitely suggest that this be a "real" conversation, either in person or via Facetime or Zoom, not a series of texts or emails. Intent and feeling are things that are not always well understood in those types of communications.

 Now, to prepare for this important conversation, we recommend that you keep the following things in mind.

1. **It is important to thank your parents for what they have done for you**. We bet that the thought exercise you did already will help you here. Chances are there are lots of things you now actively realize your parents have done and (hopefully) continue to do to support you . . . thank them for these!

2. **You want to create and strengthen a sustainable relationship**. You can tell your parents that your needs and desires are different now that you are entering adulthood and living (in many cases) on your own. This is something that means your relationship almost has to change, but it doesn't have to be tense or contentious. To that end, let your parents tell you their views and feelings, too. In other words, use your effective communication skills!

3. **Realize that they very likely don't want to lose closeness with you**. You have moved away . . . at the bare minimum in terms of your independence . . . and that can feel to your parents like they are being left behind. Part of any "nosiness" may be, for their parts, an effort to maintain the relationship. Building in some ways to maintain connection with your parents, on your terms, may be a really good thing.

4. **Be specific in your requests**. Have your lists of things you would like to be different *and* to continue (you did this earlier!), and refer to them in your conversation. Try to communicate what you want to be different would actually look like. So, for instance, if you want fewer "check-in" calls, saying "It would be cool if you would call once a week" instead of "Please just call less often" would be more effective. What behaviors can they engage in – or stop – in order for you and them both to know that they are meeting your needs as their adult child.

5. **Be reassuring.** More than anything, most parents just want to know that their kids are going to be happy and successful. While you can't guarantee that – nobody can – you can assure them that you are going to be OK. You can commit to using the resources at your school and community to get help when you need it. You can also tell them that if you really need them, you will let them know. Letting you go, so to speak, can be easier for parents if they know that you will ask for help if you are in trouble. This doesn't have to mean "saving" you; it can be advice, or just listening and being supportive.

Alright!! Take a second to make some final notes to yourself, here, about what you want to say to your parents, and how you want to say it.

_____

_____

_____

_____

_____

_____

You are ready!

☐ **Put "Schedule Big Talk" on your Task List and, when it's scheduled, add it to your calendar. Check here when you've done that**.

Good luck in your conversation with your parents. You have done good preparation to take this on. If you are working with a therapist as you do this renegotiation, you will probably be checking in about this, too, before and after the conversation. Bring your workbook with you to refer to, in that case.

Remember, it's actually pretty likely that things will not change exactly as you might want them to in the space of one conversation. All relationships are dynamic . . . they change and react as time and experience goes on. Realize that, as an adult, you are becoming a kind of partner with your parents. Make this partnership a good one, an open one . . . one that will serve you all well for the rest of your lives.

References

Buhrmester, D., Furman, W., Wittenberg, M. T., & Reis, H. T. (1988). Five domains of interpersonal competence in peer relationships. *Journal of Personality and Social Psychology*, *55*(6), 991–1008. https://doi.org/10.1037//0022-3514.55.6.991

Buri, J. R. (1991). Parental authority questionnaire. *Journal of Personality Assessment*, *57*(1), 110–119. https://doi.org/10.1207/s15327752jpa5701_13

Kurdek, L. A. (1994). Conflict resolution styles in gay, lesbian, heterosexual nonparent, and heterosexual parent couples. *Journal of Marriage and Family*, *56*(3), 705–722. https://doi.org/10.2307/352880

6 Adulting

Module 6.0   Why It Matters and Roadmap

College students often struggle with what psychologists call "activities of daily living". These *adulting* tasks require you to manage yourself and your life and they include keeping a clean and organized living space, doing laundry, grocery shopping and food preparation, managing finances, making travel/social plans, and keeping up with errands and appointments, such as going to the doctor to get a prescription renewed or renewing your car registration. You may also be working a part- or full-time job and be concerned about planning for a career.

Adulting tasks like these can be even more challenging for students with ADHD because they require organization, attention, planning, and other executive functioning skills. Adulting problems have an impact. They can make it hard to live independently, be successful at school, maintain important relationships, and feel good about yourself. Adulting problems can also cause issues in other areas. For example, not planning ahead about your meals can result in unhealthy eating behaviors and poorer physical health. Forgetting to pick up your prescription for ADHD meds means you have to deal with more symptoms. Misplacing materials for class in a messy living space can cause you to miss assignments.

But the good news is that, like other areas covered in this workbook, college students with ADHD can develop and use new adulting skills. Let's start by helping you figure out which area(s) of adulting you need to work on first.

Check Yourself: What's Your Target?

Think about each of the four major areas of adulting listed in the following and write a few sentences about how you are doing right now in each. What is going well and what's not?

Thoughts about organizing my living space and keeping it neat:

Thoughts about planning meals, social activities, and appointments:

DOI: 10.4324/9781003149620-7

> **Thoughts about managing my finances:**
>
> **Thoughts about succeeding at work and planning for a future career:**

Now, based on what you wrote, answer the following questions:
  Which adulting area is currently **causing the most problems** in your life (circle one)?

| Organizing your space | Planning meals, activities, appts. | Managing finances | Work/ Career |

Which adulting area are you currently **managing the most effectively** (circle one)?

| Organizing your space | Planning meals, activities, appts. | Managing finances | Work/ Career |

Which adulting area do you feel **most capable of changing right now** (circle one)?

| Organizing your space | Planning meals, activities, appts. | Managing finances | Work/ Career |

Looking back on your answers, which area **would you like to commit to working on right now**?
  Remember, it is okay to commit to *small changes* to start!
  I'll commit to working on:_____

Make Your Plan

1. **Put a "1" next to the module that you just wrote down** (the one you're committing to).
2. **Include any additional modules that you think might be helpful** or that you're curious about, **adding a 2, 3, or 4 to indicate your priorities.** (You <u>don't</u> need to include all the modules in your plan.)
3. **Work on the modules you selected in priority order** (1 through 4) by adding each module to your **task list and/or calendar** and tackling them one at a time. Check off each module when you finish it and **reward yourself for a job well done!**

Adulting Skills Plan

In my plan?	Done	Module	Pages
		Module 6.1. *Organizing Your Living Space and Keeping it Neat*	**140–143**
		Module 6.2. *Planning Meals, Appointments, and Activities*	**143–146**
		Module 6.3. *Managing Finances*	**146–150**
		Module 6.4 *Succeeding at Work and Career*	**150–155**

> A lot of the skills and strategies that the modules in Adulting will build on the organization and time management skills introduced in Skill 1 of this workbook. Therefore, if you haven't already gone through the modules in Skill 1, we encourage you to spend some time with those before you tackle Adulting skills.

Module 6.1   Organizing Your Living Space and Keeping It Neat

If you have selected this module, like many college students, you probably struggle with keeping your living space organized and neat. Living spaces might include your dorm room or apartment – both private and shared spaces – and your car, if you have one. In this module, you'll first choose which living areas that you want to tackle. And it's okay to start small. For example, maybe you want to start with getting your desk or work area organized so that you can be more efficient in getting school assignments done. Or maybe you want to focus on keeping the common areas of your apartment cleaner so that your roommates aren't complaining. Or maybe just cleaning the old food wrappers and receipts out of your car and putting a trash receptacle in it could go a long way to reducing your stress levels.

As you are thinking about which areas to begin with, we think it's helpful to **walk around your living spaces and take stock**. Start with your bedroom and then move into any other living spaces that you have shared or unshared. Finish by taking a look in your car (if applicable).

Write the results of your living space observations here:

Bedroom observations: _____

Work Space observations: _____

Bathroom observations: _____

Kitchen observations: _____

Living room observations: _____

Car observations: _____

Other observations: _____

Now, considering your observations, think about which areas you would like to focus on. Messy or disorganized areas are good places to start. Dirty areas are also an indication you might benefit from focusing on this area. Which of the following areas do you want to tackle? You can't do everything all at once, so you might think about which areas will have the most positive impact on your life or most reduce your stress levels.

Put a "1" next to the first area you'd like to target, followed by a "2" and a "3".

_____ Knowing where my phone and keys are
_____ Keeping up with my laundry
_____ Keeping my closet and drawers organized
_____ Keeping my bedroom organized
_____ Keeping my desk area organized
_____ Keeping important paper documents organized
_____ Keeping my electronic files (e.g., computer, Google Docs) organized
_____ Cleaning out my email inbox
_____ Keeping my bathroom and toiletries organized
_____ Doing dishes consistently
_____ Keeping the kitchen neat
_____ Keeping the refrigerator organized
_____ Keeping shared spaces clean (e.g., living room shared with roommates)
_____ Keeping my car clean
_____ Keeping my purse or backpack organized
_____ Something else: _____

Ok, now that you have selected some areas or goals to focus on, let's think about some strategies for tackling these areas. Many of these strategies build off the organization and time management skills that you learned in Skillset 1 of this workbook, so make sure you've completed that work before you continue here.

We've grouped the potential strategies into two sections: (a) keeping a clean living space and doing laundry and (b) strategies for organizing your workspace. But we will be the first to say that these lists of strategies are not all there is. There are people who make entire careers out of creating clean and organized spaces, so **you may also want to try searching the internet for specific strategies to fit your particular challenge**.

Read over these strategies and place a checkmark next to the ones that you want to try. To start with, we suggest you pick only two to three strategies, even if most of the strategies seem like they will be useful. Starting with just a few strategies will better ensure that you will be successful in implementing them and not get overwhelmed.

Strategies I want to try	Strategies for keeping a clean living space and doing laundry
	Establish a "landing pad" where you always keep important items, like your keys and wallet (e.g., a basket or hook right inside your door)
	Use an electronic tracking device system (e.g., Tile, Apple AIRTAG) to keep track of frequently misplaced items like your phone, keys, and wallet

Strategies I want to try	Strategies for keeping a clean living space and doing laundry
	Set weekly times in your calendar to: (a) straighten your living space; (b) clean your living space; (c) do your laundry
	Pair something enjoyable with cleaning tasks (e.g., We always clean our apartment on Sundays before we go out for brunch or dinner; I always do my laundry on Saturdays while watching Netflix)
	Ask your roommates to agree to a standard time for all of you to straighten and clean together (i.e., to be your accountability partners . . . and you can be theirs!)
	When doing laundry, set alarms to remind yourself to start a load in the washing machine, transfer a load from washer to dryer, take laundry out of dryer, fold, and fold and put away
	For laundry, make a chart of any special washing instructions for your clothing items and post near your washer and dryer or keep with the supplies you take to the laundromat
	Do your dishes at the end of each day instead of letting them pile up over several days; listen to your favorite music or podcast while you do your dishes, or save dessert until after you have done your dishes as a reward
	If you have the money, consider hiring a cleaning service for a one-time deep cleaning to get you started.
	Use time cracks (remember these?!) to clean or straighten your living space
	Do one cleaning task daily rather than saving them to do all at once so it is less of a burdensome task (e.g., Monday is laundry, Tuesday is vacuuming, Wednesday is cleaning the bathroom). Put these tasks on your calendar and task list
	Reward yourself for successes in these areas. For example, a week of doing your dishes daily = a movie night with friends
	Another strategy I've identified:

If your goals involve improving the organization of your home workspace or office, check out the strategies for that, given here. Put a checkmark next to the ones that you want to try. Again, select only a few strategies to begin with. You can always try more strategies later.

Strategies I want to try	Strategies for organizing a home workspace or office
	Set weekly times in your calendar for organizing home workspace or office
	Have a daily routine for this task (e.g., I always straighten my desk before I start my homework)
	Make sure that you have an area for doing homework that isn't used for other things (e.g., don't put your clean laundry on your desk where you need to do your homework)

Strategies I want to try	Strategies for organizing a home workspace or office
	Make sure you have materials in your homework area that you might need so that you can be more efficient when you sit down to work (e.g., paper, pens, laptop charger cord, calculator)
	As a general rule of thumb, don't turn one task into two (e.g., after you fold your laundry, put it away immediately rather than putting it on your desk where you will have to move it before you can start your homework)
	Use a filing system (a drawer or even a banker's box) to organize important documents, like your apartment rental agreement, passport, academic documents, instructions booklet for TV.
	Re-organize your electronic documents into folders and subfolders on your computer
	Another strategy I've identified:

Go for It!

Now that you have selected your goals related to organizing your living space and keeping it neat and you have selected a few strategies to start with, it is time to implement your strategies. Put these goals and strategies into your task list and calendar, think through your plan, and get started with the first steps.

☐ **Check here when your goals and strategies are in your task list and calendar**.

Once your new strategies are in place, you can reevaluate your goals and determine whether you have made progress. If the strategies you selected to implement first do not seem to be working or are too difficult, go back to the previous charts, and pick some new strategies to try.

Module 6.2 Planning Meals, Appointments, and Activities

If you selected this module, you're having difficulties with planning for important non-school things that happen in the future. For example, like many college students, you might not see your doctor or dentist regularly and then scramble for an appointment when there's a problem. You might let your driver's license, passport, or car registration lapse, which might mean a period of not driving or traveling, or could result in expensive tickets. You might wait to schedule a haircut until your hair is out of control, only to find that there are no appointments available. And maybe you miss out on travel or social opportunities with friends because of not planning ahead. If this sounds like you, don't worry – like everything else in this workbook, there are skills that can help.

For many college students, with and without ADHD, parents are providing major help in managing appointments and travel. However, these adulting activities are important for you to master to become more in control of your own life. Planning meals and grocery shopping are key adulting tasks that have important benefits. If you grocery shop regularly and plan for meals, you will eat out less and likely be more healthy and have more money to do other things.

The first step is to **set goals** around which areas you would like to change related to planning meals, appointments, and activities. Your goals might include some of the following:

- I want to plan, cook, and eat more healthy meals at home.
- I want to schedule and remember to attend yearly doctor and dentist appointments and monthly haircut appointments.
- I want to pay my taxes, renew my car registration, and pay my bills on time.
- I want to plan my holiday trips to see family more in advance to get the best travel times and prices.
- I want to schedule a fun activity with friends once every week and try a bunch of new activities.

Using the space given here, list out two to three goals like these you would like to start with:

Goal 1: _____

Goal 2: _____

Goal 3:_____

Now that you have created some goals, here are some strategies for achieving those goals. Place a checkmark next to the strategies you would like to try first, keeping in mind that it's better to start with just a few new strategies. Then, after you have evaluated whether these strategies worked, you can try some more. As with the other adulting areas, many of the suggested strategies build off the organization and time management skills that you learned in Skillset 1 of this workbook. So, if you haven't worked through Skillset 1 yet, this would be a good time to do that.

Strategies I want to try	Strategies for successful grocery shopping and food preparation
	Set weekly times in your calendar for grocery shopping and food preparation; consider keeping these times the same each week to establish a routine (e.g., grocery shopping Sunday morning followed by food preparation Sunday afternoon)
	Grocery shop 1–3 times per week by planning for a few days in advance
	Make a grocery list before you go to the store; organize your list by aisle if you always shop at the same store (recommended to make shopping more efficient) to avoid forgetting items in going back and forth
	Begin with a base list of things you need each week (e.g., milk, bread, coffee) and add to it things that are specific to that week
	Lean on electronic helpers. Some online recipes will add items to a grocery list for you, and some grocery stores will let you make a list online that you can re-use weekly (e.g., Paprika).
	Look for "meal of the day" or "meal of the week" specials at your grocery store. Some stores will have a recipe card and all the ingredients needed at the front. Others will have meal specials (e.g., a rotisserie chicken and two sides) that are pretty healthy and easy to prepare

	Buy pre-prepped foods to make food preparation easier (e.g., pre-washed salad greens, pre-chopped veggies, pre-cooked meats). Note: These are not the same as ready-to-go meals (e.g., frozen dishes), which tend to not have as much nutritional value and also tend to be expensive
	Remember that you can gain efficiency and time by preparing meals that are big enough to have leftovers. Consider starting with one thing that you can make on the weekend and then eat throughout the week (e.g., make a pan of lasagna and divvy it into single serving size containers that you can eat throughout the week)
	Recruit roommates, friends, or significant others as accountability partners for meal planning or prep. Invite friends over to have a "meal prep party".
Strategies for scheduling errands and appointments	
	Pick a month (e.g., August right before school starts, December/January between semesters) when you schedule your yearly doctor and dentist check-ups; put scheduling these appointments on your calendar for two months before the month in which you'd like to have the appointment.
	Put all appointments on your calendar, set a reminder or notification 1 week and 1 day before the appointment. You can also put expirations for driver's license, car registration, and passport on your calendar with reminders to renew before the expiration date
	When you are at an appointment that you need to have regularly (e.g., haircut, doctor to pick up prescription), schedule your next appointment and immediately put it on your calendar
Strategies for managing travel or social plans	
	Put your travel dates on your calendar at the start of the semester
	Let your family members and/or significant other know your dates/plans
	Determine whether you need to book flights or make storage arrangements and put those tasks on your to-list and calendar if needed
	Early in the week, think about plans you would like to make for the weekend (e.g., go to a football game or party with friends, meet with a study group, hike or bike with friends)
	Decide when you would like to contact your friends about these plans and either send them a text or chat message or put it on your list of things to do for a specific day of the week

 Strategies for healthy eating and meal preparation are covered in more detail in Module 4.2, so be sure to check out that module if you set a goal related to improving your eating here.

Go for It!

Now that you have created your goals related to planning meals, social activities, and appointments and you have selected a few strategies to start with, go ahead and implement your strategies.

☐ **Check here when your goals and strategies are in your task list and calendar**.

If the strategies you selected to implement first do not seem to be working or are too difficult, go back to the table and pick some new strategies to try.

Module 6.3   Managing Finances

If you have selected this module, you are likely interested in making some improvements in how you manage your money. Take a few minutes to think about the current state of your finances. Here are some questions to ask yourself:

- Do you have a budget for your expenses?
- Do you often pay monthly bills (e.g., rent, cell phone) late?
- Do you keep up with your account balances?
- Do you often run out of money before the end of the month?
- Do your parents get frustrated because you end up asking for more money?
- Do you manage your own finances and pay your own bills/taxes or do your parents do it for you?
- Do you have credit card debt?

Even if you are having problems in most of the areas described earlier, you are not alone. Many college students have problems with managing their money – there is often too little money and too many fun things to spend it on! Add to that the problems in executive functioning that we know college students with ADHD face, and it is not surprising that many students with ADHD report having problems with managing their finances.

For many college students, parents essentially manage their finances. This might include paying monthly bills, adding money monthly or semesterly to a spending account, paying credit card debt, and filing taxes. For other students with ADHD, parents may be involved with some, but not all, of these financial tasks. An important goal of young adulthood is to become more independent so that you can control your own life, so even if your parents are willingly and successfully managing your finances now, it's important for you to move toward managing this task independently. In this module, we offer a number of strategies for successfully managing your finances.

Build a Budget

A big step toward successfully managing your finances is to build a budget. We recommend that every student starts here. A budget is a financial tool that will allow you to plan and track your income and spending over a period of time, typically monthly. It is a great way to keep up with your monthly expenses and to reduce overspending. Developing a budget may also help you save up for big purchases (think ski trip with friends, new video gaming system). Later in your life, having a budget can help you with saving money for a house, a car, a family, or retirement.

Usually, a budget for a college student is pretty straightforward. We have provided a **student budget worksheet** on page 148 for you to use to get started. In the longer term, though, we suggest using Microsoft Excel or a free Smartphone app such as Mint, Goodbudget, Everydollar, or Buddy to create your budget and track your expenses. The Smartphone apps are really nice because they are portable and allow you to keep track of your expenditures as they occur.

Let's go through the steps to create your budget:

1. <u>Gather up your financial paperwork and electronic files.</u> First, you're going to do an **audit.** This is where you get a sense of how things are for you financially; that is, how your income and expenses compare. To do this you need to gather utility/rent/insurance bills, bank statements, credit card statements, paystubs, and receipts from the last three months. Basically, you want to pull together any information that will help you determine how much money you have coming into and going out of your accounts each month.

2. <u>Calculate your monthly income.</u> This includes money you get from working, from parents, from student loans, and other sources. Some of this may come to you semesterly, rather than monthly. If it does, just divide the semester amount by 4.5 (usually the months in a semester) to calculate your monthly "income". **Put this information in the first blank column of the worksheet under "Where I am".**

3. <u>Make a list of your monthly expenses and determine fixed and discretionary experiences.</u> Next on the worksheet, use your bank and credit card statements, receipts, and bills from the last three months to determine your monthly expenses. These expenses might include rent or mortgage payments, car payments, insurance, groceries, utilities, entertainment, personal care, eating out, transportation costs, travel, or savings. Fixed expenses are often *needs* and are ones that stay the same each month that you pretty much have to pay, like your rent, cell phone bill, car insurance payment, and money for groceries. Discretionary expenses are *wants* that may change monthly or are more optional, like eating out, gifts, media subscriptions, and entertainment. Go ahead and determine a monthly spending amount for both your fixed (*needs*) and discretionary (*wants*) expenses. For discretionary expenses, you can average your spending in each category over the last three months to help nail down a total. **Calculate totals for fixed and discretionary and then add them together to get your total expenses**.

4. <u>Compare your monthly income and expenses.</u> At the bottom of the sheet, subtract your expenses from your income. **If your income is higher than your expenses**, you are in good shape. You can put the extra money aside for savings, use it to pay off debt, or for special one-time spending (like attending a concert with friends, a big gift for your significant other, textbooks at the beginning of a semester, or a donation to a good cause). **If your income is lower than your expenses**, this means that you are overspending and need to make some changes. Look at your discretionary expenses for places you can cut. For example, you might be able to eat out less each month, cancel memberships you are not using regularly, bike to school instead of driving, or reduce spending on entertainment. If this is not enough to balance your budget (balanced is when expenses = income), you may need to examine your fixed expenses and make cuts there. For instance, you may need to find a less expensive rental apartment or advertise for a roommate to share expenses. Or, you may need to get a part-time job or take out a student loan to bring in more income.

5. <u>Set your goals.</u> Now you're going to make your budget! In the **Where I want to be** column, plan out your goals in terms of income and expenses.

6. <u>Effectively use your budget.</u> Once you have set up your budget, you must regularly monitor and track your expenses in each category, ideally each time you pay a bill or make a purchase. This is where having a free budgeting app really comes in handy as it is always with you on your phone and you can immediately record your expenses. You can also add "recording expenses/evaluating your budget" to your weekly calendar and task list to keep up with these important activities regularly.

Recording what you spend throughout the month will help prevent overspending and help you understand your spending patterns and where you might be able to cut, if necessary. As you use your budget, keep an eye on how much you have spent in each category. Once you meet your monthly limit in that category, you will have to either stop spending in that category for the rest of the month or move money from another category to cover expenses. For example, if you have reached your monthly budget for eating out by the third week of the month, you may need to prepare your own food for the last week of the month to ensure you do not go over your budget. Or, if it is really important to you to eat out during that week, you may have to reduce the money you spend that week on other types of entertainment or on gas for your car. Overall, your goal in using your budget should be to keep your monthly expenses less than or equal to your monthly income. Finally, circumstances change, so be sure to update your overall budget regularly, and certainly any time you have a major change in your income or expenses (e.g., you move to a new apartment with a different rent amount, you get a second job, you join a new gym).

7. On the worksheet, you should <u>repeat your audit at the end of the following month</u> in the **Where I ended up** column and take stock of your progress. What went well and where do you need to adjust your strategy? You can always use additional copies of the worksheet or a budgeting app to continue the work.

Student Budget Worksheet

	Where I am	Where I want to be	Where I ended up
	Audit for month of:	*Budget Goals*	*Audit for month of:*
Income			
Wages			
Family Contribution			
Grants/Scholarships			
Loans			
Withdrawals from Savings			
Misc. Income			
Total Income (add rows above)			
Fixed Expenses – Needs			
Tuition and Fees			
Rent/Housing			
Utilities			
Cable/Internet			

Laundry			
Groceries/Meal Plan			
Car Payment			
Car Insurance and Registration			
Gas/Transportation			
Car Servicing			
Parking			
Credit Card Payments			
Cell Phone Plan			
Books and Supplies			
Prescriptions and Medical Expenses			
Other:			
Total Fixed Expenses			
Discretionary Expenses – Wants			
Eating Out			
Entertainment			
Clothing			
Cabs/Rideshare			
Gym/Hobbies			
Personal Grooming			
Other shopping			
Travel			
Other:			
Total Discretionary Expenses			
Total Expenses (Fixed + Discretionary)			
Income Versus Expenses			
Total Income (from above)			
Total Expenses (from above)			
Income minus Expenses			
Savings or Deficit? (+ or −)			

Other Strategies for Managing Finances

In addition to building and sticking to your budget, there are some other useful strategies for managing your finances and ultimately becoming more independent in this area of adulting. Read over the strategies in the following table and place a checkmark next to the ones you would like to try first.

Strategies I want to try	*Strategies for Managing Your Finances*
	Put bill paying and reviewing your finances on your calendar monthly
	Always pay your credit card bill in full or use a debit card instead (see https://vimeo.com/199334296) to avoid paying interest.
	Review your bank and credit card statements once a month; use the online banking feature which often includes an app where you can access account information quickly and easily
	If you have the money, pay ahead several months of bills at one time
	If your parents provide you with money every month and you often run out before the next installment, ask your parents to send your money weekly rather than monthly
	Set up automatic bill pay through your bank or utility companies for recurrent and predictable expenses (e.g., cell phone bill, car insurance, rent)
	Save up for big expenses, like a vacation, by setting aside a little money in a savings account each month. You can set this up to automatically occur through your bank
	If you have trouble following through on these tasks, find an accountability partner, such as a significant other or parent, who might be willing to physically sit with you (in-person or by Zoom) while you complete these tasks

Go for It!

Now it's time for you to set up your budget using the steps in this module and to implement the additional strategies you selected to manage your finances.

☐ **Check here when your strategies and steps of your plan are in your task list and calendar**.

If the strategies you selected to implement first do not seem to be working or are too difficult, go back to the table and pick some new strategies to try.

Module 6.4   Succeeding at Work and Career

College will end . . . eventually. And for many people the next step will be to devote a good portion of their time to their career. In this module, we'll help you work through some things you can do right now to function better in any jobs you currently have (or will have in the future). Then we'll invite you to "think big" and consider which career pathways might best fit your strengths and your interests in a way that can work with your ADHD instead of against it. Finally, we'll give you some information about when and how to consider requesting workplace accommodations in line with the Americans with Disabilities Act (ADA).

What Do Employers Want?

In order to develop job skills, it's important to know what employers are actually looking for. A survey of employers by the Collegiate Employment Research Institute identified six reasons they had fired recent college graduate employees and seven things that had made them give people promotions (Gardner, 2007).

Review the following charts and give yourself a "grade" for each skill. Then choose the one, two, or three areas that you think you should work on first.

How to Keep Your Job	*What grade would you give yourself (A-F)?*	*Place an "x" in front of the areas you think you should work on most.*
Behave ethically		
Display motivation and work ethic		
Use technology appropriately on the job		
Follow instructions		
Show up for work and show up on time		
Complete assignments by their deadlines		
How to Advance in Your Job		
Take initiative to complete tasks and solve problems		
Self-regulate and self-motivate		
Display a positive and flexible attitude		
Show commitment and passion for the work		
Motivate others toward common goals		
Communicate clearly and persuasively		
Demonstrate technical knowledge and competence		

Now that you have identified some areas to develop, it's time to think about which skills you've been working on throughout this workbook could help you out. For example:

- Paulo gives himself a "good grade" for taking initiative, but admits that he often does not follow through on these commitments by his employer's deadline. He decides to focus on adding these deadlines to his calendar and not taking on any new tasks at work until all prior tasks are completed.

- Angie isn't always truthful about "clocking in" accurately at work because she's worried she'll get in trouble with her boss for showing up late – which has been happening often. Angie decides to commit to being honest with her boss in the future and sets up a meeting to tell her about the strategies she plans to use to get to work on time, such as adding pre-programmed alarms to her phone.
- Greg loves working with customers at the front desk at his job, but when things are "slow", he struggles to stay off of his phone and has gotten reprimanded by his boss twice for it. He decides that he will turn his phone off and put it in a drawer in another room during his work shifts. He also decides to ask his supervisor for other work tasks to do during slow times, which he thinks will demonstrate his initiative to help out.

Now it's your turn. Use the following table to focus on each job skill you want to work on, the skills from this workbook that can help you succeed, and the steps you'll take in the next week. Be sure to check off each action when you've added it to your calendar and task list.

Job Skill to Work On (From Table Above)	*Skills That I Can Use*	*Modules or Page Numbers for These Skills*	*Specific Action I'll Take This Week*	*Check Here When Added to Calendar or Task List*

What Do **You** Want?

In the previous section, we focused on the skills that employers look for in successful employees. In this section, we invite you to look ahead and think about what it is YOU want out of your career. Research has shown that career "fit" is especially important for people with ADHD (Lasky et al., 2016). Many adults with ADHD report that the impact of their symptoms depends a lot on the situations they are in and so choosing the right work environments can promote better performance and well-being.

Lasky and colleagues (2016) interviewed adults with ADHD and found that many of them preferred their work to be challenging, novel, fast-paced, hands-on, and interesting. Work that is interesting can help promote focus and follow-through, and so choosing a career field that fits both your interests and your strengths (and not your weaknesses) can contribute to success and satisfaction in the long term.

Check out the following (fictional) example to illustrate a bit more what we mean.

Justin's Story: To Ski or Not to Ski

Justin's favorite job so far has been his work as a ski instructor. He enjoys helping people improve their technique and learn to love the sport. Every client is different and he gets satisfaction from figuring out how best to help each person. He likes that no two days are ever the same and that he gets to interact with other people who love skiing. His challenges on the job have been similar to his other ADHD-related challenges in college – showing up on time and keeping his schedule straight – but he's been able to improve on that by using his calendar, task list, and alarms on his Google Calendar.

However, Justin's dad doesn't think that being a ski instructor is a good career path and instead is strongly encouraging Justin to study accounting and work in his family's small accounting firm. Justin has always sort of assumed that this will be his path but recently he's considering whether this type of work setting is the best fit for him. He doesn't find the work very interesting and he has trouble focusing at a desk for long periods of time. He finds that his ADHD symptoms seem to really get in the way of his success. Justin has never thought of his ski instructor job as a viable career option, but after a conversation with his roommate about his lack of interest in accounting, he decides to set up an appointment at the Career Services center at his college to discuss some options. He may not be a ski instructor forever, but maybe there are opportunities in the world of skiing (a multi-billion dollar industry!) or other careers with similar characteristics where he could thrive.

Like Justin, you might be able to identify some characteristics of work settings that interest you and might work well with your strengths as well as your ADHD-related challenges. And, like Justin, it may be hard to think of how these characteristics might fit into a career that can support you financially or a career that seems to fit with others' expectations for you. But, at this point, we invite you to stay open to exploring some possibilities using the following prompts.

What kinds of work settings and tasks do you think might be a good fit for you? In other words, where do you like to work, with whom, and what kinds of tasks are engaging and meaningful to you? Are there any areas or activities that have kept you motivated in the long term?

_____

_____

_____

_____

_____

Can you identify any specific jobs or careers that might be a good fit for you? This is just exploratory! If you need some help, you can visit www.123test.com/career-test/ to explore what kinds of careers might fit the bill. List your ideas here:

_____

_____

_____

_____

Now, you're going to <u>take all of this to the career experts</u>!

Next, set up an appointment with your college's career services office to discuss the notes you just made. You can likely find their contact information and how to make an appointment by searching the college website. If your college doesn't have a career services office, you can set up an appointment with your academic advisor who can help direct you. **<u>Do this now</u>** and put it in your calendar and task list!

Location of Career Services Office: _____

Date and Time of My Appointment: _____

Name of Career Services Person (if available): _____

**Add a reminder to bring this workbook and your notes to the career services session.

□ **Check here when this information is added to your calendar and task list**.

Accommodations . . . at Work?

As a college student, you may be familiar with classroom accommodations designed to help you access your education. (If not, check out the Introduction to this workbook or Module 2.5 for more information.) These accommodations are provided in compliance with a federal disability law, the ADA, and are designed to provide equal access for those with and without disabilities. The law also applies to many (but not all) employers and workplace settings. If some aspect of the work or work setting creates a barrier to a worker with a disability, the worker can request, in ADA terminology, a *reasonable accommodation*.

Importantly, requesting an accommodation requires the worker to disclose their disability status (but not a specific diagnosis) and to take the initiative to request the accommodation. If you would like to consider requesting a workplace accommodation, we recommend the following steps:

1) Carefully review these resources about accommodations in the workplace and how they apply to people with ADHD:
   a) https://adainfo.us/accommodations
   b) https://chadd.org/adhd-weekly/asking-for-workplace-accommodations/
2) Think Through: When does my ADHD get in the way at work?
3) Think Through: Which *specific supports* could I request to lower these barriers while still getting the job done?
4) Plan Out: How will I disclose my disability and request my accommodation? Consider framing your request from a position of strength versus weakness: For example, instead of, "I will get distracted less if X", try, "I believe I will be even more productive if X". Communication skills in Skillset 5 might be helpful here!

Happy Working!

References

Gardner, P. (2007). *Moving Up or Moving Out of the Company? Factors That Influence the Promoting or Firing of New College Hires* (Research Brief No. 1–2007). Collegiate Employment Research Institute. https://ceri.msu.edu/_assets/pdfs/young-pro-pdfs/Moving-Up-Moving-Out.pdf

Lasky, A. K., Weisner, T. S., Jensen, P. S., Hinshaw, S. P., Hechtman, L., Arnold, L. E., W. Murray, D., & Swanson, J. M. (2016). ADHD in context: Young adults' reports of the impact of occupational environment on the manifestation of ADHD. *Social Science & Medicine, 161*, 160–168. https://doi.org/10.1016/j.socscimed.2016.06.003

If You Need More Help With ADHD . . .

We hope that you have seen some significant improvements in your daily life after working your way through this workbook! However, if you are still having difficulties in some areas of your life, you are not alone. Despite their best efforts, some students with ADHD may find it hard to work through the skills by themselves without guidance from a professional. Other students may have applied many of the skills suggested in this workbook, but are still struggling with a particular area of functioning.

If you haven't improved as much as you'd like from working through this workbook by yourself, it may be beneficial for you to work with a professional. A counselor or therapist can help you apply the skills in this workbook using the companion **therapist guide** for *Thriving in College with ADHD: A Cognitive-Behavioral Skills Approach*.

Additionally, a mental health professional can provide more targeted therapy for certain areas that you have identified as a problem. For example, if you are still having trouble with your sleep even after working through Module 4.1 (Sleeping Better), a counselor could help you work through Cognitive Behavioral Therapy for Insomnia (CBT-I), which is an evidence-based treatment developed specifically for insomnia. Finally, we know that many college students with ADHD have other mental health difficulties besides their ADHD – things like anxiety or depression – that can make it difficult to learn and apply the skills in this workbook. Working with a mental health professional to address these other areas of difficulty might make it easier for you to learn and apply the skills in this workbook.

Finding a Counselor or Therapist

If you have decided to seek the services of a mental health professional, here are some suggestions for identifying counselors or therapists in your geographic area:

- Check out your college or university's Student Mental Health Center. Many centers offer several individual or group counseling options that are included with your student health fee. Some may even offer ADHD-specific coaching or therapy. **Hint: most campus mental health services are within the general Student Health Center, so start your search there.
- Reach out to your college or university's Office of Student Disability Services. Although they likely do not offer counseling themselves, they may have a list of resources for students both on campus and in your community.
- The Association for Behavioral and Cognitive Therapies (ABCT) offers a "Find a Therapist" tool on their website: Find a CBT Therapist – Association for Behavioral and Cognitive Therapies (abct.org)

- Psychology Today also offers a "Find a Therapist" tool: <u>Psychology Today: Health, Help, Happiness + Find a Therapist</u>
- Check out the website for CHADD, a national advocacy group for children, adolescents, and adults with ADHD: <u>CHADD – Improving the lives of people affected by ADHD</u>. On this website, there are links for a Resource Directory, ADHD Center Directory, and an online support community for adults with ADHD.
- Look for a website for your state's psychological association. Many state psychological associations offer a Directory of psychologists in the state that is searchable by zip code.
- If you are having trouble finding a therapist in your community or want the convenience of virtual therapy, check out BetterHelp: <u>BetterHelp – Get Started & Sign-Up Today</u>

Index

Locators in **bold** refer to tables and those in *italics* to figures.

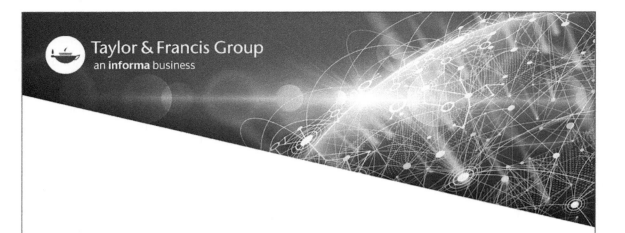